Get Grea
Information
Fast

Get Great Information Fast

JOHN GERMOV
AND
LAUREN WILLIAMS

Allen & Unwin

First published in 1999 by
Allen & Unwin
83 Alexander Street,
Crows Nest NSW 2065 Australia
Phone: (61 2) 8425 0100
Fax: (61 2) 9906 2218
E-mail: info@allenandunwin.com
Web: www.allenandunwin.com

National Library of Australia
Cataloguing-in-Publication entry:

Germov, John.
    Get great information fast.

    Includes index.
    ISBN 1 86448 536 1.

    1. Database searching. 2. World Wide Web (Information
    retrieval system). 3. Library orientation. 4. Information
    retrieval. I. Williams, Lauren. II. Title.

025.04

Set in 10/12 pt Plantin Light by DOCUPRO, Sydney
Printed in Australia by McPherson's Printing Group

10 9 8 7 6 5 4 3 2

Contents

Figures and tables

Figures

Tables

Handy hints

Preface

This book stems from our passionate belief in the need for students to develop skills in learning as well as knowledge. It is the book we wished we had when we were students because the ability to find relevant and credible information is an essential skill, and this is especially so in a world now dominated by information technology. This book is for students in all academic disciplines and is a companion to John Germov's (1996) *Get Great Marks for your Essays* (Sydney: Allen & Unwin). Both books aim to provide the essential skills that students require but aren't necessarily told about. We have written this book both as lecturers who deal with students and as ex-students ourselves; as such, we appreciate the need for all students to have a quick reference guide to finding great information fast.

We would like to thank the following people: Jane a'Beckett for her unfailing assistance with many aspects of this book; Steve Campitelli for his marvellous illustrations; Jane Potter, for finding information for us; Jan Williams, for proofreading chapters; our publisher, Elizabeth Weiss, who first suggested we write this book and provided us with constant support and encouragement; Marj Kibby and Marcus Smith for their insightful comments on the web chapter; and Peter Diplaris for suggestions on using people as sources of information. Thanks also to our partners Sue Jelovcan and Greg Hill for their support and understanding. Finally we are grateful to our students who inspired us to be better teachers through their helpful feedback over the years.

John Germov and Lauren Williams
The University of Newcastle
June 1999

How to use this book: Finding what you need fast

- *Do you find it difficult and time-consuming to obtain the information you want? Do you even know where to begin?*
- *Would you like to know how to use World Wide Web search engines and CD-ROMs to provide relevant sources of information?*
- *Do you quickly become immersed in information-overload, without knowing how to manage, organise and evaluate what you find?*

This book aims to address all of these questions by meeting the needs of students in any discipline, whether at university, college, TAFE or senior secondary school. Based on our own experiences as teachers and students, we have developed this book by anticipating your questions and providing plenty of handy tips and practical advice to give you the knowledge and skills to find the information you want quickly and effectively.

We have all heard enough cliches about living in the 'information age' and 'surfing the information super-highway' to last a lifetime. This book provides a clear and simple guide through all the hype and helps you to develop your information literacy skills. Preparing essays, reports, presentations, debates and seminars is a reality of student life. Success in these tasks depends on finding useful information and finding it fast.

This book is designed for anyone who needs to search for information, manually or electronically. We cover the most common issues and problems you may encounter when searching for information. The book has a user-friendly format:

* Each chapter starts with questions commonly asked by students, which are then answered through practical examples and handy hints.
* Key terms are bolded in the text, with definitions provided in a glossary.
* An appendix provides a comprehensive list of web sites that should meet all of your information needs.

Get Great Information Fast has two aims:

1 to give you the skills to find the information you want
2 to show you the process of how best to do this.

Therefore, you can use this book in two ways: either by reading it from cover to cover and conducting your information search as you go along, or by dipping into relevant sections and using the book as a directory and memory jogger.

Get Great Information Fast not only gives you the skills to determine and find the information you need, it also shows you how to evaluate what you find so that you become a critical user of information. Along the way, we show you many time-saving tips to make your quest for information— and, more importantly, knowledge and understanding —simpler, more effective and more rewarding.

This book also has its own web page, with a list of starting-point web sites to make your quest for information easier. Visit the *Get Great Information Fast* web page at
http://www.allen-unwin.com.au/study/infofast.htm
You can also provide us with feedback on the book through this site.

1 The information quest: The search for life, the universe and everything

- *How do you decide what information you need?*
- *What basic sources of information exist?*
- *What's the difference between information and knowledge?*

Asking the right questions: Determining what information you need

> *The Answer to the Great Question Of . . . Life, the Universe and Everything . . . Is . . . Forty-two.*
>
> Douglas Adams (1979) *The Hitch-Hiker's Guide to the Galaxy*, London: Pan, p. 135.

The key to finding the right answer to any question is to have a clear understanding of the actual question in the first place. As the above quote shows, such a task is not always as simple as it appears. We often embark on our search for information knowing very little about the actual topic. As a student you are constantly being introduced to new concepts, facts and theories. Such a steep learning curve means that you need to be careful not to go 'off-track' in your search for information. The answer to the question of 'life, the universe and everything' shows that you can waste a lot of time searching for information that is useless if you fail to work out *exactly* what it is you are looking for and the best means to find it. In other words, you need an information plan. This chapter will introduce you to a simple step-by-step method which will save you time and guarantee that you get great information fast. However, before we introduce you to the plan, you need to have a clear understanding of the type of information that exists and how to turn information into knowledge.

What is information?

We seek information to be enlightened, to be aware and to find out about a particular topic, person or event. There are two basic types or sources of information: primary and secondary.

1 **Primary sources** are the original sources of information—creative work, research data collected from interviews, surveys and experiments as reported in journal articles, books and research theses, reports (annual corporate financial statements, minutes of meetings, government reports), new concepts and theories. The primary source of the information is the person, group or organisation that actually created the information in the first place. Many academic disciplines require you to use primary sources to ensure that you have accurate and reliable information. The old joke about the 'catch of the day' illustrates why: one person tells another that they caught a sizeable fish, then that person tells another and another and another . . . until, before long, the fish has become a whale! To avoid exaggeration, misinterpretation and other errors, it is important to use primary sources.
2 **Secondary sources** are summaries, reviews, discussions and analyses in the form of textbooks, review chapters and articles, and reference works such as encyclopaedias, dictionaries, handbooks and manuals. Secondary sources

do not create new data, but collect several primary sources of information in one piece of writing and attempt to explain, analyse, synthesise, clarify and disseminate that information.

Primary or secondary sources—which should you use? The answer depends on what you want to achieve. If you are writing an in-depth essay on a specified topic, you would use both. It would be helpful to start with secondary sources, since primary sources can be difficult to understand, difficult to locate, out of date and only provide a partial understanding of a particular issue. This is where secondary sources can help by providing an overview and basic understanding of a topic. However, it may be difficult to judge whether the information contained in a secondary source is accurate and valid. For example, it is possible for a secondary source to be biased or to misinterpret primary source material. To avoid bias and misinterpretation, it is essential that you go to the original, primary source of information. A golden rule to follow is: always survey the whole field of literature on a topic and never base your conclusions on just one source of information, whether primary or secondary.

The ability to survey the literature has been made easier with developments in **information technology** (IT) which have revolutionised how we find and access information by giving us sources such as on-line library catalogues, **CD-ROMs** (Compact Disk Read Only Memory) and the World Wide Web (**WWW**). Most primary and secondary sources of information are now compiled, categorised or indexed via at least one of these electronic means. A large portion of this book is devoted to showing you how to extract information from various forms of information technology.

On being sceptical: Bridging the information–knowledge divide

There is a subtle difference between information and knowledge. Information exists as an entity and refers to some form of descriptive or factual data. Knowledge, however, refers to how you understand that information and incorporate it into your world view. You can be drowning in information, but *know* very little if you cannot understand, evaluate and apply the information you have. To turn information into knowledge requires you to become sceptical and critical of the information you uncover. In many ways you need to become an information detective or 'info-sleuth'; seeking not only to find information, but also to determine its accuracy. How can you believe the information you find? The answer to this question is specifically addressed in Chapter 8, but in general it is worth applying the following questions to information you find:

- Is the information relevant to the topic?
- Is it up to date?

- Is enough detail provided?
- Does the author have a vested interest in producing the information?
- Does the author provide supporting evidence for any claims made?
- Does alternative or conflicting information exist?
- How does the information relate to what you already know?

By keeping these questions in mind, you guard against biased and partial representations of the topic you are investigating. The main way to address the potential of bias is to seek multiple sources of information rather than relying on one source for all of your information. You also need to consider who produced the information and whether this may bias the content. For example, the official unemployment rate for a country may be 8 per cent of the population—this is information. However, there may be significant dispute over the accuracy of official statistics. For example, many commentators have noted that 'hidden unemployment' exists due to assumptions made in the collection of unemployment statistics. Furthermore, the point of view as to whether the information of an 8 per cent unemployment rate is accurate or not might vary between politicians in government and those in opposition.

We should take nothing for granted because information presented as 'fact' can often change over time, vary between cultures, be altered according to emphasis and depend to a large extent on interpretation. Therefore, information that may at first glance appear fairly innocent and uncontroversial may be otherwise if we adopt a sceptical approach. We are surrounded by plenty of factual information describing events—such information is often the basis of media reporting. For example, information about who won a political election seems uncontentious. However, there may be more to 'the facts'. Suppose there were allegations of vote-tampering—an important piece of information that may be left out of some

HANDY HINT 1: On the importance of being sceptical

The old saying 'you can't believe everything you see on TV' can be applied to the media in general. While we all know this saying, many of us depend on television for our daily news and current affairs. However, in the search for stories, even the media can be duped, as occurred in the mid-1980s in Australia. The local version of '60 Minutes' (a current affairs program) put the media to the test. They invented a psychic named 'Carlos the Channeller' in the mould of the famous Uri Geller (who, in the early 1980s, did the talk-show circuit amazing audiences with his 'powers' of mind-reading and spoon-bending). Carlos' (fictitious) management group sent out media kits with made-up stories from major news outlets and publicity material promoting his forthcoming 'tour' of Australia.

Within a week of sending out the media kits, one TV program decided to scoop everyone else and arranged a satellite interview with Carlos from the United States. This required '60 Minutes' to employ an actor to fly to America for the interview! By the time Carlos arrived (back) in Australia, other media outlets wanted to pick up the story. After a series of interviews, Carlos was invited on a popular TV breakfast program during which he acted out a stage-managed publicity stunt where an argument with the presenter resulted in Carlos throwing a glass of water over one of the interviewers and storming off stage. This incident made front-page news and Carlos became a household name. Stories and interviews with Carlos appeared in every major newspaper, TV and radio news program. So successful was this publicity that Carlos was able to hold a free public meeting at the Sydney Opera House—it was a full house, as thousands had come to hear him speak!

The point of this story is that the media were so easily duped and manipulated because not one reporter had bothered to check the background of Carlos. If they had checked with US news correspondents or followed up on one of the fake US newspaper reports included in the media kit, the whole con game would have collapsed like a house of cards. Therefore, the moral of the story, to borrow a phrase from 'The X-Files' TV series, is 'trust no-one'. You don't have to be paranoid, but simply be sceptical, knowing that information can be false, biased, incomplete, poorly researched, misinterpreted and misunderstood.

factual accounts. Therefore, discrete pieces of information may be deceptive unless they are interpreted, questioned and put in context (see HANDY HINT 1 for an example).

The famous philosopher Socrates is recorded as saying that he was only sure of one thing in life—that he knew nothing—and from this assumption he set out to learn about the world by never presuming he had all the answers or a complete understanding of any issue. Therefore, the point we wish to make is that there is a distinction between information and knowledge. Knowledge is your under-standing and explanation of 'why things are as they are', rather than simply stating or presenting certain information as fact. Only by accessing a number of information sources on a topic can you guarantee the accuracy of the information you gather. If you keep these issues in mind you will translate information into knowledge; that is, you interpret and eval-uate the information you gather.

Where to begin? Using an Information Search Plan

It is tempting to jump straight into the task of finding information by rushing into the library or accessing the **Internet**. However, the lack of a plan is the first mistake those on the information quest make. By constructing a basic plan, which only takes a short time, you will save plenty of time in the long run by avoiding confusion, unnecessary diversions, dead-ends and poor-quality information. The Information Search Plan (ISP) provides a systematic format to organise your thinking and information-gathering on a topic. The remaining chapters of this book take you through the key stages of the ISP in-depth; however, a brief overview of each stage is provided below.

1 Define and interpret the topic: Using the funnel technique

The most important part of searching for information is to clearly define and interpret your topic. You can only start to look for information once you have a basic idea of what it is you are actually looking for. By spending a little time interpreting and clarifying your topic, your Information Search Plan begins to take shape. This will guide your further research. Chapter 2 will show you some effective strategies for this first step, such as conducting preliminary reading of introductory material and identifying the scope of the information to be sought by addressing the questions of who, what, where, when and why. This is particularly helpful when you know very little about a topic and are not even sure where to begin.

2 Determine keywords for searching

Once you have interpreted the topic, you should have a basic idea of the content of the information you need. The next stage of the plan is to determine keywords to use in your further information search, such as key concepts, theories and authors. We suggest the **mind map** technique as a handy tool in doing this in Chapter 2.

3 Select information databases to be searched

To get great information you will need to know how to use a library, whether it be an actual library or a **virtual** one. You need to be aware of the way your library catalogues its materials, the various resources it holds and the ability it has to access inter-library loans if it doesn't have the items you seek. There are many catalogues, indexes and CD-ROM databases covering a variety of disciplines which allow you to search for keywords on your topic to identify books, journals, conference reports, audiovisual material and web sites. Chapter 3 will introduce you to the key features of libraries to help you become familiar with the resources and information databases available.

4   Conduct the search

While information technology has improved our ability to find and access information, the sheer quantity of information available has produced its own problems. It is easy to waste considerable amounts of time wading through unnecessary and irrelevant material due to the range of databases available—this is why you need to know some effective search tips. Chapters 4, 5 and 6 show you how to search effectively using on-line catalogues, CD-ROMs and the Internet.

5   Organise the information sources you find

After retrieving several sources of information as a result of your searches, you will need to organise them in some way so that they don't get lost. Chapter 7 shows you how to organise your notes and manage the information in a way that suits your style.

6   Information retrieval

Once you have found potential sources of information, you now need to start building that information into knowledge. Chapter 8 shows you how to read academic sources of information and how to use the 'skimming technique' to quickly determine if a particular source of information is relevant. Depending on the quality of the information located, you may need to review and refine your keywords and conduct a further search if necessary.

7 *Make effective notes and evaluate your information*

Chapter 8 provides some simple techniques to make and organise useful notes. We also discuss how to evaluate the information you have gathered. As we argue in this chapter, it is not enough just to gather bits of information. You need to interpret, synthesise and assess the quality of the information you find and turn it into knowledge.

8 *Reference your information*

Chapter 9 shows you how to reference the information you have gathered, including how to reference the Internet. Practical examples are given of three key referencing systems: Harvard/APA, footnotes and Vancouver. The final chapter provides an overview of the ISP process and offers some suggestions for applying the information you have found to specific written assignments.

The next chapter shows you how to interpret a topic, determine the scope and type of information you need to collect, and construct a mind map of your information search.

2 Starting-point: How to define and interpret your topic

- *How do you interpret a topic?*
- *Where is the best place to look for information?*
- *What is mind mapping and how can it help you to search for information?*

Before you rush into searching for information on a topic, you need to spend some time interpreting that topic. This is particularly important when a topic is new to you. In this chapter we introduce two handy methods for interpreting topics—the funnel technique and mind mapping. This is the starting point of your information quest and the first stages of your Information Search Plan (detailed in Chapter 1).

The funnel technique

The funnel technique involves finding some basic information to gain a general understanding of the topic. From this general starting-point, you can narrow your search down to the more specific information required for your topic. Imagine a funnel as depicted in Figure 2.1. At the top of the funnel are sources of information that provide a basic,

Figure 2.1 The funnel technique of interpreting your topic

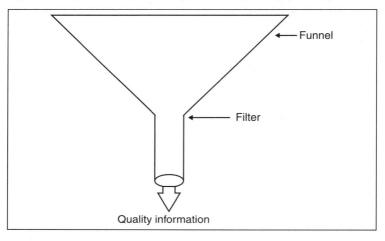

general and broad understanding of your research topic. As you progress down the funnel, you accumulate more information, narrowing your search and finding the specific information you need, filtering out the quality information relevant to your task at hand.

The top of the funnel

The key places to start looking for information to help understand and define a topic are:

- your lecture notes, introductory textbooks and prescribed reading
- reference works: encyclopaedias, general dictionaries, discipline dictionaries and bibliographies
- personal interviews: people can be useful information sources
- archives, museums, art galleries and memorials (where relevant)
- review articles and chapters.

Use your judgment as to which of these are relevant to your topic. We will now look at each source in more detail.

Lecture notes, introductory textbooks and prescribed reading

An obvious place to start looking for general information is your lecture and/or course notes. If the topic has already been covered in the subject you are studying, then your lecture/course notes will provide you with some basic idea of what key terms, concepts and authors to search for. Your teacher may have also provided you with a subject guide, set a textbook, and listed some prescribed reading or relevant references. While these materials are unlikely to provide you with all the information you need, they have been provided for a reason—you would be wise not to ignore them.

If you are searching for information in a particular discipline area—whether it be agriculture, economics, sociology or biochemistry—introductory texts are a good place

Table 2.1   Keyword examples by discipline

Academic discipline	Keywords for set assignments
Agriculture	animal husbandry, cloning, breeding, 'Dolly' (the cloned sheep)
Biology	genetics, ecology, biotechnology
Economics	gross domestic product, balance of payments, monetary policy
Sociology	socialisation, social structure, social closure, cultural capital
Biochemistry	mutation, DNA repair, nucleotides
Psychology	dreams, psychoanalytic theory, Sigmund Freud

to begin. While their comprehensiveness will vary, textbooks provide convenient summaries of information on particular topics in terms that are easy to understand. Whenever you are about to research a topic, you should always locate a number of textbooks (for up-to-date material, make sure they have been published recently) and check the contents and index pages for anything relevant to your topic. If you are unclear about exactly what your topic entails, flip through chapters or sections of books that are in the 'ball park' in terms of your topic. In this way, you can get a better understanding of what your topic is about. Make a note of any **keywords**—such as concepts, authors and theories (where relevant)—that are used. Keywords act as signposts when you search for more information. See Table 2.1 for some examples of keywords for specific topics.

Reference works
All libraries have a reference section that includes works such as reference guides (see HANDY HINT 2), atlases, dictionaries, telephone directories and directories of professional, business and government organisations. Other reference works which can be particularly helpful in your quest for information are:

- encyclopaedias
- discipline dictionaries
- subject bibliographies

HANDY HINT 2: Using reference guides to find reference material

If you are unsure of the range of reference material available in your area, you can consult the following volumes, which are guides to reference books:

- *Walford's Guide to Reference Material: 1996–1998*, 7th edn, London: Library Association Publishing (most university libraries should have copies):
  Vol. 1. *Science and Technology*, edited by Marilyn Mullay and Priscilla Schlicke
  Vol. 2. *Social and Historical Sciences, Philosophy and Religion*, edited by Alan Day and Michael Walsh
  Vol. 3. *Generalia, Language and Literature, the Arts*, edited by Anthony Chalcraft, Ray Pryterch and Stephen Willis.
- Herron, N.L. (ed.) (1996) *The Social Sciences: A Cross-disciplinary Guide to Selected Sources*, 2nd edn, Englewood: Libraries Unlimited.

- biographical directories
- yearbooks, handbooks, manuals, maps and atlases.

There are many general and specialised encyclopaedias that you can use. Encyclopaedias can be useful for summarised information about a topic; however, you should not rely solely on them, as often the material can be too general, out of date and biased towards the country in which the encyclopaedia was published. Some examples of the range of encyclopaedias available are:

- *Encyclopaedia Britannica* (various years and volumes), Chicago: Encyclopaedia Britannica.
- Hook, B. (1991) *The Cambridge Encyclopedia of China*, 2nd edn, Cambridge: Cambridge University Press.
- *The 1995 Grolier Multimedia Encyclopedia*, Version 7.0, Danbury: Grolier Electronic Publishing.

- Kahn, A.P. and Hughey Holt, L.L. (1992) *The A-to-Z of Women's Sexuality: A Concise Encyclopedia*, revised and expanded edn, Alameda: Hunter House.

English dictionaries contain definitions of words in their everyday usage, whereas discipline dictionaries contain words and terms that have a specific meaning within the context of that discipline. Examples of discipline dictionaries include: politics, history, biology, medicine, industrial relations, environmental studies, sociology and psychology. These dictionaries are a good starting-point in clarifying and interpreting a research topic by providing brief summaries of concepts, theories and theorists, and often references for further reading and other related information.

Subject bibliographies are lists of references that have been published on specific authors or topics. They may be organised by date, author or type of publication. Often such publications are annotated bibliographies, with short descriptions 'annotated' to each entry explaining what the publication is about. Such books can be helpful where detailed historical and analytical material is needed on a particular author or topic. For example:

- Johnson, D.L. and Fallon, M.S. (1981) *18th and 19th Century Architecture Books and Serials in South Australia: A Bibliography and Research Guide*, Adelaide: Libraries Board of South Australia.
- Klimasauskas, C.C. (ed.) (1989) *The 1989 Neurocomputing Bibliography*, 2nd edn, Cambridge, MA: MIT Press.
- Brockwell, C.J. (1979) *Aborigines and the Law: A Bibliography*, Canberra: Law Department, Research School of Social Sciences, ANU Press.
- Farley, J. (1982) *Academic Women and Employment Discrimination: A Critical Annotated Bibliography*, Ithaca: New York State School of Industrial and Labor Relations, Cornell University.

Biographical directories are national and international lists of prominent people in various industries such as government, business, professions, entertainment and the arts. They are useful for basic descriptive information about people (their position, achievements, and so on) and, in some cases, their contact details. The most well-known examples of such directories are the 'Who's Who' publications, such as:

* Information Australia (1998) *Who's Who in Australia: An Australian Biographical Dictionary and Register of Prominent People*, 34th edn, Melbourne: Information Australia.

However, there are often specific publications for particular industries and professions. These directories provide brief descriptive accounts—biographies—of the people they list. For example:

* Cattel Press, Jr (1984) *Who's Who in American Art*, New York: Bowker.
* Blaug, M. (1986) *Who's Who in Economics: A Biographical Dictionary of Major Economists, 1700–1986*, 2nd edn, Cambridge, MA: MIT Press.

Such directories are helpful for finding detailed information about specific people and their contributions to a particular discipline.

Yearbooks, sometimes referred to as almanacs, are collections of statistical and descriptive material on countries, specific subjects and significant events over a twelve-month period. For example:

* South African Communication Service (1996) *South Africa Yearbook*, Pretoria: The Service.
* Australian Stock Exchange (1995) *The Australian Stock Exchange Yearbook*, Sydney: Australian Stock Exchange.

Such publications can be useful for basic statistical information and often include references to other relevant publications which provide more detailed statistical information.

HANDY HINT 3: Info-sleuth tools of the trade

To make the information quest easier, it is worthwhile purchasing your own copies of the following reference sources:

- An *English dictionary*: for definitions and to check pronunciation and spelling.
- A *thesaurus*: a dictionary of similar words that can provide you with alternatives for keyword searches and generally help to spruce up your writing. Note that most word processing packages also provide this facility.
- A *discipline dictionary*: to provide the specific meaning of terms used in your particular discipline, which can vary considerably from their literal meaning in everyday usage. They are especially useful for identifying keywords for further searches.
- A *style manual*: provides information on how to write and reference material for authors in a particular discipline. Some common style manuals include:
  - Australian Government Publishing Service (1994) *Style Manual for Authors, Editors and Printers*, 5th edn, Canberra.
  - Peters, P. (1995) *The Cambridge Australian English Style Guide*, Melbourne: Cambridge University Press.
  - Gibaldi, Joseph (1995) *MLA Handbook for Writers of Research Papers*, 4th edn, New York: Modern Language Association of America.
  - Gibaldi, Joseph (1998) *MLA Style Manual and Guide to Scholarly Publishing*, 2nd edn, New York: Modern Language Association of America.
  - American Psychological Association (1994) *Publication Manual of the American Psychological Association*, 4th edn, Washington, DC.
  - Strunk, W. and White, E.B. (1979) *The Elements of Style*, 3rd edn, New York: Macmillan.

— Iverson, Cheryl et al. (1998) *American Medical Association Manual of Style: A Guide for Authors and Editors*, 9th edn, Baltimore: Williams & Wilkins.

Handbooks and manuals tend to be practical and vocationally-oriented reference guides, explaining procedures and standards in particular disciplines and professions. For example:

* Ronalds, C. (1991) *Affirmative Action and Sex Discrimination: A Handbook on Legal Rights for Women*, 2nd edn, Sydney: Pluto Press.
* Harnsberger, H.R. (1995) *Handbook of Head and Neck Imaging*, 2nd edn, St Louis: Mosby.

People as sources of information
If you can't get the information you are seeking from written sources, you may need to contact people directly for information. People can point you in the right direction in terms of searching for information and clarifying issues and may even provide you with relevant information. Some companies and government departments have telephone information lines to answer your queries. However, you should exercise caution when the main role of the person you are contacting is not to act in response to public enquiries. This doesn't mean that people will be unwilling to help you, but it does mean that you need to approach them in a considered and thoughtful way. To maximise your chances of success, we suggest the following strategies:

1   *Be specific in your request*
Consider the following scenario:

A busy university academic, who specialises in the area of public health nutrition and is doing research on women and dieting, gets a phone call one day from a TAFE student that goes something like this: 'Hi, I'm doing an assignment on the nutritional needs of vegetarian athletes. Someone gave me your name. So, can you send it to me?' 'Sorry, can I send what?' 'Whatever you've got on vegetarian athletes.' After recovering from shock, the academic explains to the student that there is a whole process to go through in order to find information. The moral of this story is that busy people won't appreciate non-specific requests or being asked to do your work for you. On the other hand, the same academic received a call from a student doing Honours in English in the area of the social pressure on women to diet, who asked about information in this area from the nutritional science perspective. This request was quickly and enthusiastically responded to, because it was specific and relevant to the person whose help was being enlisted.

Therefore, the moral of the story is to make sure you know enough about your topic to ask specific, intelligent questions. Never say, 'Can you give me everything you've got' on a certain topic; and remember that academics and other professional people are not your personal research assistants.

2   *Be considerate*
The person you are phoning is likely to be busy, so always ask whether it is a good time to talk. (The scenario described above was made worse by the fact that the academic had several people in their office at the time and was trying to have a meeting.) Even better than phoning is using **e-mail** if you have access to it. Most university and government department web pages have e-mail addresses listed for staff (see Chapters 5 and 6).

3   *Try to make your request relevant to the other person*
A friend, working as a marketing consultant with a market research company at the time, tells a story about a phone

enquiry from a student who persistently requested a detailed list of market research data. Such companies exist to earn money by charging for their services, and the student was told: 'This isn't the ABS, mate!' With the commercialisation of many government services, even the ABS (Australian Bureau of Statistics) now charges for its services, so be aware that people you are calling may be under this 'time is money' pressure. First ask whether the department you have contacted has any information about the topic that you might purchase.

4   *Be appreciative*
Basically, when you are phoning a person for information, you are asking them for a favour. Thank them appropriately. If they have really gone out of their way to help you, a letter to their manager acknowledging that fact would be appropriate.

Archives, museums, art galleries and memorials
Depending on the discipline, relevant information can be found in many actual sites that archive or display artefacts for public access. For example, the National Archives of Australia indexes and stores original Commonwealth government records, such as documents on immigration, defence, foreign affairs and the findings of Royal Commissions. There are also personal papers of past government officials, maps, photographs, films, radio and TV broadcasts. Many commercial organisations also keep archives and may make them available to researchers or the general public through exhibitions. Furthermore, key public buildings such as memorials, galleries and museums should not be overlooked as sources of information.

Narrowing the funnel: Using the references of other authors

After consulting a number of general sources as discussed above, you can use these as the base from which to 'springboard' on to more detailed sources of information. It is always good practice to make a note of the sources used by authors writing on your topic. For an instant list of further information on a topic, look up the references cited in the material you have already found. These provide a springboard to other relevant sources. For example, note and locate the references cited in the relevant section of intro-ductory texts. Not all of the sources in reference lists will be useful or relevant, so you will need to judge their relevance based on the date and place of publication, the title, and the importance given to them in the text of the material where they have been cited.

Review articles and chapters

One of the best ways of applying the springboard technique is by using review articles and review chapters. It is fairly common for reviews of the literature on key topics to be published regularly and these make for a substantial 'spring' into the other relevant information sources. The author of a review article provides you with a systematic overview of a specific topic. By definition, the references will be a list of original (primary source) material on a topic. For example, imagine you are preparing an essay on the role of ultraviolet radiation in the causation of cancer, and you come across an excellent article that reviews the results of several studies called 'The contribution of ultraviolet radiation to the devel-opment of cancer'. Do not fall into the trap of only using the review article to discuss the studies themselves. You will need to go to the primary sources (the original studies) so as to be able to discuss them in detail in your essay. (And you must never reference the primary sources as if you have looked them up when you have only relied on the review. Markers can tell!) Furthermore, there are Annual Review journals for most disciplines that collect reviews together. In Chapter 4 we discuss how to find relevant journals and journal articles. Here again you need to be careful not to rely on only a few sources of information or you are in danger of missing some relevant material or presenting a biased viewpoint.

The funnel as a filter: Asking who, what, where, when and why/how

Once you have a basic understanding of your topic, it is important to further specify the scope of information you require by asking 'who, what, where, when and why/how' questions, such as:

* *Who*: Do you need to know about specific individuals and/or organisations?
* *What*: How detailed does your information need to be?
* *Where*: Is location important, such as regional, country specific, international or comparative information?
* *When*: Are dates important? Does the information need to be historical or current?
* *Why/how*: Do you need to address explanations, analyse information and come to conclusions? The 'why' or 'how' question is a key aspect of university study and, if answered well, it is where higher marks are gained. The 'why' part will determine whether your information needs to be descriptive and/or analytical, which will influence the way you go about searching for information. Depending on the topic and discipline area, you may need to consider information that addresses the 'how' question. That is, you may be required to explain how a particular event occurred or how something works.

Be discipline-specific

A further consideration is the academic discipline in which you are working. For example, for information on unemployment, there are various types of information we can seek: descriptive statistics on the rate of unemployment, further breakdowns of the unemployment rate by age, region, industry, state, country, over time, ethnicity and gender. We may also be interested in public policies on unemployment and explanations of the causes of unemployment and possible solutions to the problem. Different academic disciplines will approach a topic from their own perspective, so it is important to keep this in mind when searching for and evaluating the information you find. To continue with the example of unemployment, a range of academic disciplines would approach the topic in different ways—for example:

- *Economics*: the economic costs of unemployment.
- *Psychology*: the effect of unemployment on depression.
- *Health sciences*: the relationship between unemployment and health.
- *Sociology*: the social causes and effects of unemployment.
- *Philosophy*: why the paid work we do defines our lives.
- *Politics*: the role of political policies and interest groups in addressing unemployment.
- *History*: how historical employment trends and past public policies impact on present unemployment rates.

Thus, the discipline base can significantly affect the nature of the information you find, and so you will need to be familiar with the perspective of your own discipline to ensure that you get relevant information.

The info-search mind map

You can address the questions of 'who, what, where, when and why/how' in a list or by using the mind map technique. Have you ever been involved in a brainstorming exercise— where you write the ideas of a group down on paper or on a whiteboard? Mind mapping is simply brainstorming on your own. To construct a mind map, you start with a clean sheet of paper and draw a circle in the middle of the page about the size of the base of a small drinking glass. In that circle, you then write the central idea or theme of the essay

Figure 2.2   Mind mapping a psychology essay on Freud's theory of dream analysis

Figure 2.3   An essay mind map unfolds

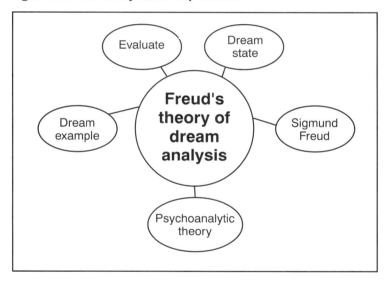

or report for which you are seeking information. Figure 2.2 shows the beginnings of a mind map for a psychology essay on the following topic: 'Evaluate Freud's theory of dream analysis and give an example of how the theory works using an actual dream.'

Next, draw a series of lines radiating out from this

Figure 2.4 Adding further detail to your mind map

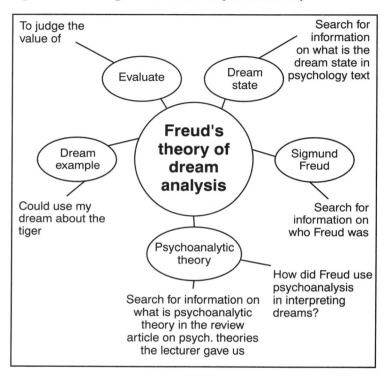

central circle or bubble. At the end of each line, write a key word, term or concept related to your central topic which you will explore further in your search. For example, you might look back on your lecture notes and find that Freud is credited with developing psychoanalytic theory, so add this to your mind map. The important thing with a mind map is to jot down the thoughts as they come to you. There is no particular order and a mind map should not be hierarchical (see Figure 2.3).

Now you are ready to search for each of these key terms and concepts in turn. You can use your mind map to plan this search by jotting down potential sources of information on the map (see Figure 2.4). The dream example is something you could search for based on your own memories of dreams or those of your friends. To understand the word 'evaluate', you might go no further than a dictionary. This will lead you to a meaning of the term which is 'to judge the value of'. Thus, you know that in your essay you will not only be required to describe Freud's theory of dream analysis, but also to judge the value of that theory. For example, you will need to explain how Freud's theory has contributed to the broader field of dream analysis. Then you will need to do further searches on the other three bubbles —dream state, Sigmund Freud and psychoanalytic theory.

After you have completed your mind map, you have a plan of how you will search for information. Keep it handy for later—you may need to add to it after you have finished the next few stages of your Information Search Plan.

Now that you have interpreted your topic and have mind mapped the information you need, the next chapter deals with how to begin your search in the library.

3 Getting the most out of your library

- *What are the essential things I need to know about using my library?*
- *How is information catalogued in a library?*
- *What should I do when I know the books I want are in the library, but are missing from the shelves?*

Once you have obtained a broad understanding of your topic and determined some keywords for a detailed search, as discussed in the previous chapter, it is time to conduct your information search. The main sources of information are the books and journal articles found in libraries. This chapter will explain how library material is organised so that you can make the best use of library catalogues and resources.

Get to know your library

Whether your library is a multi-storeyed university library or a single-room municipal library, the biggest mistake you can make is not knowing how to get the most out of that facility. Larger libraries usually conduct orientation tours to show you where certain types of information are kept and

the range of material and information databases the library has. These tours are free and informative, so make the most of this service. While a general orientation tour is essential, it is worthwhile to do a follow-up tour to refresh your memory and catch up on new library developments— particularly additions to electronic information databases.

For information between tours, libraries usually provide helpful written guides on how to use their services. Some libraries even produce discipline-specific leaflets that contain a list of key sources of information which can be useful as a good starting-point for your information search. The other important thing to note is that librarians are very helpful people. If you have tried several means to find information and failed, then by all means ask for help. However, respect the fact that librarians are also busy people and don't ask them to do things you could do yourself.

What about using other libraries?

Don't restrict yourself to the one library, as it may not provide sufficient material to suit your needs. The most obvious libraries for researching information are university libraries. These will vary according to the size of the university and the type of courses offered. Some universities also specialise in certain topics, such as rare books and archival documents, or may have specialist libraries such as medical and law libraries. Therefore, depending on the information you are seeking, you may need to consider using other university libraries if they are within reach. Remember, university libraries are public institutions and therefore you don't have to be a student of a particular university to use the resources within its library (though you may not have access to borrowing rights). State and national libraries are also great public resources and, along with university libraries, can be used as virtual libraries through the World Wide Web (see Chapter 5 and the appendix for details).

How books and journals are stored: The Dewey and Library of Congress classification systems

The great beauty of libraries is that they all use similar systems for organising their material. Most library material is either organised using the Dewey Decimal classification system or the Library of Congress classification system.

The Dewey system

In the Dewey system, material is catalogued by decimal 'call numbers' that are assigned to particular topics. The listings for the major Dewey Decimal categories are given in Figure 3.1.

The call numbers are further specified by decimal points—for example, 192.12—which are used when there are many books on a particular subject or when a new, very

Figure 3.1   The Dewey Decimal classification system

000–099	Generalities	500–599	Pure sciences
100–199	Philosophy	600–699	Technology/Applied sciences
200–299	Religion	700–799	The Arts
300–399	Social sciences	800–899	Literature
400–499	Language	900–999	Geography & History

The ten categories are further subdivided into more specific categories—for example:

100–199	**Philosophy**
110	Metaphysics
120	Epistemology, Causation, Humankind
130	Paranormal phenomena
140	Specific philosophical viewpoints
150	Psychology
160	Logic
170	Ethics
180	Ancient, Medieval, Oriental
190	Modern Western philosophy

specific listing is required. In some cases, letters may also be used, for example, 182.23/ARN, to further differentiate individual library items. In most instances, the letters refer to the first part of the author's surname. Figure 3.2 shows how library material catalogued using the Dewey system would look when placed on library shelves.

Journals are also listed by title in the Dewey classification using the same alphanumeric system, usually with the prefix 'S' to indicate a serial publication. (Some libraries use 'P' for periodical or just plain 'J' for journal.) For example, *The Australian Journal of Politics and History* can be indexed as 'S909.8205', and *Scientific American* as 'S505/8'. You should also be aware of Quarto collections, which are simply books and reports that are physically too big to fit on a normal library shelf. These items may be given the prefix of 'Q' for Quarto to indicate that they are held in a separate section of the library. All libraries also have a Reference collection, where material is designated by the abbreviation 'R' or 'REF' and is usually not for loan. As described in the previous

Figure 3.2 Call numbers of books on a library shelf based on the Dewey system

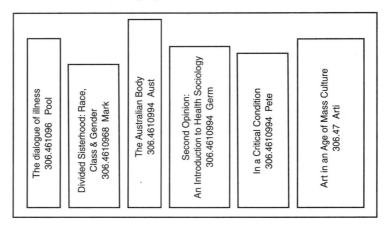

chapter, sources in the reference section of a library can be extremely useful for interpreting a topic.

The Library of Congress system

The other major system of cataloguing library material is that developed by the Library of Congress (LC) in the United States. The LC is the national library of the United States and exists primarily to service the research needs of the US Congress. However, the LC claims to be the world's largest and most comprehensive library and it is therefore a great source of information for researchers from around the world. Several Australian universities use the Library of Congress system to catalogue their material. Figure 3.3 illustrates the LC classification system which is an alpha-numeric system, based on 21 categories of alphabetical letters. The LC system can be further subdivided by a second letter, then a numeral and, if required, a combination of letters and numerals—for example, LA71.A5.

The basic LC classification system has numerous sub-

Figure 3.3   The Library of Congress classification system

A	General works	M	Music and books on music
B	Philosophy/Psychology/Religion	N	Fine Arts
C	Auxiliary sciences of history	P	Language and Literature
D	History: General & old world	Q	Science
E–F	History: America	R	Medicine
G	Geography/Anthropology/Recreation	S	Agriculture
H	Social sciences	T	Technology
J	Political science	U	Military science
K	Law	V	Naval science
L	Education	Z	Library science

classes as shown in Figure 3.4. As this sample shows, the LC system is very detailed and idiosyncratic.

The on-line catalogue

The classification systems are used to organise books and periodicals physically within the library. Lists of these library holdings are catalogued on large computer databases which tell you where the materials are located in the library. The on-line catalogue lists all the library holdings, such as books, journals (but not journal articles), multimedia (audiotapes, videotapes, films, CD-ROMs), reference material, archival material and, in some cases, web page addresses. The on-line catalogue will also note if the material is available in hard copy, or in some other medium such as microfiche, CD or on the World Wide Web (WWW). The on-line catalogue contains the bibliographical details of a library's holdings, such as author, title, publisher, place of publication, edition (if relevant), year of publication and type of publication (book, journal, conference report, audio-cassette, audiovisual, CD-ROM) and the catalogue number that represents an item's position on the library shelf. If you know the author or title of the work you are searching for, you enter these in the on-line search. However, there will be times when you want to search a whole category to get a list of what

Figure 3.4 **A sample of Library of Congress sub-classes taken from category H: Social sciences**

H	
1–99	Social sciences (general)
HA	
1–4737	Statistics
29–32	Theory and method of social science statistics
36–37	Organizations. Bureaus. Service
38–39	Registration of vital events. Registration
154–4737	Statistical data
154–155	Universal statistics
175–4737	By region or country
HB	
1–3840	Economic theory. Demography
71–74	Economics as a science
75–130	History of economics
131–145	Methodology
135–145	Mathematical economics
201–206	Value. Utility
221–236	Price
238–251	Competition. Production. Wealth
501	Capital. Capitalism
522–715	Income. Factor shares
531–551	Interest
601	Profit
615–715	Entrepreneurship. Risk and uncertainty
801–843	Consumption. Demand
846–846.8	Welfare theory
848–3697	Demography. Vital events
3711–3840	Business cycles. Economic fluctuations

specific material is available. Then you simply enter words to search for items so that the computer can scan for an exact match in the library catalogue. Keywords, sometimes called descriptors or simply subjects, are also included in the on-line catalogue. These are often derived from publications such as the Library of Congress Subject Headings (LCSH) and the Medical Subject Headings (MESH) publications. These terms can be used to search the on-line catalogue.

Most on-line catalogues allow you to narrow or broaden your keyword search by using **Boolean** search techniques which we describe in Chapter 4. When you search for a particular subject or even a specific item, the catalogue may also provide a list of related subjects which you can use as alternative keywords for further searches. You may also be able to limit your search using dates (for example, over the past five years) or the format of material, such as searching for videos and audio-cassettes on a particular topic. However, the library catalogue is not the only electronic means to find information. While it will show the titles of all books and journals in the library holdings, to find information on individual journal articles you will need to access separate on-line or CD-ROM indexes and abstracts. Detailed information on conducting these searches is given in Chapter 4.

Missing from the shelves?

You've done the hard work of locating a book or a journal, using an on-line library catalogue that clearly indicates the book should be on the shelf, only to find that, no matter how hard you stare at the point on the shelf where it should be, it is nowhere in sight. There may be a number of explanations for this:

- In some libraries, new books first go to the 'new acquisitions' area for a few weeks before being placed on the shelves.
- For journals there may be a current issue section, where the most recent issue of a journal is first displayed before being placed in its proper place on the shelf.
- Many libraries at the end of the year begin to bind individual copies of a journal over the previous year into one annual volume. You can check with library staff if this is the case and when it is likely to be available.
- It is possible that the book or journal may have been slightly misshelved, so check the surrounding area.

- A book or journal may have just been returned and may be sitting on the sorting shelves, waiting to be placed in its appropriate place.
- Re-check the catalogue number just in case you copied it incorrectly.
- Finally, it may be missing. If you have tried all of the above searches unsuccessfully and think a book or journal is missing, inform the library staff so that they can look into it and order a replacement copy if possible.

The limits of information technology: A plea for browsing the shelves

By knowing the classification system used by your library, you can browse the particular shelves in the library that relate to your topic for other titles that may not come up in your search. For example, if you are looking for a book on 'ethics', you can go to the 170 call number category in the Dewey system and look at the titles of other books nearby on the shelf which might not have come up in your search due to obscure titles or incomplete databases. Sometimes, this is a simple way to locate general books on a topic about which you know very little or to search for ideas on an interesting topic to investigate. This is not a romantic yearning for the pre-computer days, but a practical result of the fact that the titles of many books remain obscure, and can therefore be missed in on-line searches despite your best efforts. Similarly, if the topic you are researching is a current issue in your discipline, then you should go to the most recent issues of one or two key journals in the area on the shelves. Use the contents pages to scan back over the last few issues for relevant articles and editorial comments.

Once you have retrieved a number of books and journals from the shelves, you need to quickly scan them for relevance. Read the back cover (or dust-jacket) of the book for a brief summary of the contents. Always read the foreword, preface and/or introduction of the book to check what it is about, its intended audience, the level of depth and difficulty, and even the approach adopted by the author. For journal articles, read the abstract, introduction and conclusion to determine the relevance of the information it contains.

The next chapter specifically illustrates how to search for information contained in academic journals using electronic means.

4 Effective search tips for finding journal articles

- *How do I search for journal articles?*
- *How can I save time searching via on-line and CD-ROM databases?*
- *How can I find high-quality information?*

Increasing amounts of information are available in electronic form accessed via a computer terminal. In this chapter we will look at finding information about journal articles—the main primary source material. When journal articles are printed, summary details are also recorded on index and abstract databases, the printed versions of which have existed for some time. However, the computer age has revolutionised these databases and we focus on the electronic versions of indexes and abstracts such as those available on CD-ROM and via the World Wide Web. Before we explain these electronic databases, it is worth clarifying why it is important to use journals in the first place.

Why use journals?

Academic journals provide the main form of primary source material. As noted in Chapter 1, primary sources are where

HANDY HINT 4: Beware—not all journals are equal

The great benefit of academic journals is that they are peer-reviewed—that is, prior to publication every article is sent to (usually) three independent academics to review its quality. While this process is not foolproof, it does mean that the information provided in journals is likely to be accurate and properly substantiated. However, it is important to remember that not all journals follow this procedure. Be careful not to confuse magazine and newsletter publications with academic journals. For example, publications such as *The Women's Weekly*, *Times*, *Newsweek*, *The Bulletin* and *Business Review Weekly* are not scholarly sources of information. Neither are the newsletters produced by many organisations. While such sources may be consulted for various reasons, they are not as credible or authoritative as academic journals and should not be used as the main source of your information.

original material is recorded in the form of creative work and new findings and theories. Journals can be published on an annual, quarterly, bimonthly or monthly basis, and are generally the most up-to-date sources of information in a field of study. While there are a number of multi-disciplinary journals, most journals are discipline-based, some very specifically, and some are directly linked to professional associations. For example:

- *Australian Journal of Nutrition and Dietetics* (journal of the Dietitians Association of Australia)
- *Psychology Today* (journal of the American Psychological Association)
- *Journal of Sociology* (journal of The Australian Sociological Association)
- *Food Australia* (journal of the Australian Institute of Food Science and Technology).

Most libraries have a 'current journals area' where the latest issue of each journal the library holds is displayed. If you are unsure about the range of journals specific to your discipline held by your library, go to this section to get an idea of what's available and what current debates are raging by scanning the contents pages of the relevant journals. Some journals will periodically print an index of their contents over the past year or five-year period which can be helpful in a search. While academic journals are viewed as credible sources of information, see HANDY HINT 4 to find out why not all journals are equal.

What are indexes and abstract databases?

As mentioned in Chapter 3, the **bibliographic** details of journal articles—such as the author, date, title, volume, issue and page numbers—are not covered by the general library catalogue. To find journal articles relevant to your topic, you need to consult publications referred to as index and abstract databases. Indexes are directories that provide the full bibliographic details of journal articles, usually for a particular discipline or topic area. Abstracts are also directories, but, as the name suggests, include an abstract or paragraph summary of each journal article they list. So when you search a topic and find an article, you can read the summary and decide whether the article is relevant to your search. If it is, you can record the bibliographic details. Indexes and abstracts exist for almost every discipline and can be kept by a library in a number of forms:

- printed hard-copy versions
- microfiche
- CD-ROM databases
- on-line databases accessed via the web.

Hard-copy and microfiche versions of indexes and abstracts were the main way of searching for journal arti-

HANDY HINT 5: What is a CD-ROM database and how does it differ from an on-line database?

A CD-ROM is similar to a music CD except that the information it contains is visual rather than audio. CDs have the advantage of holding large amounts of information and being easy and fast to use. While CD-ROMs are used for storing index and abstract information, they are also used for encyclopaedias and dictionaries (some with full audiovisual capabilities).

It is worth noting that on-line databases and CD-ROM databases are not the same thing. On-line databases are accessible via the web or an organisation's internal communication system (such as an intranet or Telnet). On-line databases are able to be updated regularly (usually weekly) and thus provide the most recent information that is available. CD-ROMs are static sources of information and cannot have additional information added to them after publication. While they are accessed electronically via a computer, the information on CD-ROMs will date in a similar way to hard-copy books and journals.

cles in libraries until the 1980s. While they continue to exist, the most convenient way to search such sources is through information technology using CD-ROMs and on-line databases. Libraries are increasingly providing access to CD-ROMs via the library's web site. This has the added benefit of multiple user and 24-hour remote access, known as using a 'virtual' library (that is, having use of the library facilities without actually being there). However, it is important to note that these indexes and abstracts do not involve searching the actual web, but are simply databases accessed through the web (see HANDY HINT 5). Chapter 5 deals with conducting effective web searches.

Major indexes and abstract databases

The first stage in on-line searching is deciding which database to search. An index exists for almost every discipline, so it is not possible to produce a comprehensive list here. However, Table 4.1 provides an overview of some of the major **index and abstract databases** available in many university libraries. Availability usually depends on the courses offered at a particular university.

Most electronic databases allow you to search for relevant journal articles in a number of ways. The databases can be used in a similar fashion to on-line library catalogues (discussed in Chapter 3). You can search by author, title and keyword. You can also limit your search request by journal title, subject area, language (that is, search for articles in English only) and by date (for example, you can search for matches to your query between 1996 and 1998).

Keyword searches

The most common way of searching for journal articles is by keywords. Once you have determined your keywords (as discussed in Chapter 2), it is often best to use more than one term to further specify your search so that you obtain material of higher quality and relevance. When your keyword searches involve more than one term, you need to use **Boolean operators**, named after the British mathematician George Boole. Boolean operators are three simple command words used to limit or broaden a search:

- AND: narrows the scope of a search to a combination of specific items by retrieving only items with both terms.
- OR: broadens a search by commanding the retrieval of items with both or either term.
- NOT: limits a search by excluding terms.

Examples of the use of Boolean operators are provided in Figure 4.1.

Table 4.1   Major index and abstract databases

- ABI/INFORM: international database of business and management citations and abstracts for articles in over 1000 journals, including the full text of over 500 journals.
- ABN (Australian Bibliographic Network): a multi-disciplinary database of all the library material contained in over 700 major Australian libraries.
- AMED (Allied and Alternative Medicine): covers acupuncture, homeopathy, Chinese medicine, hypnosis, podiatry, herbalism, occupational therapy and osteopathy.
- APAIS (Australian Public Affairs and Information Service): produced by the National Library of Australia, covering social sciences, humanities, current affairs, law and economics. Includes journals and relevant newspaper and magazine articles.
- ART Index: international coverage of art history, films, painting, photography and related fields.
- AUSTGUIDE: an index of brief abstracts from a number of periodicals including *Australian Geographic*, the *Bulletin*, *Discover*, *Far Eastern Economic Review*, *Geo*, *New Internationalist*, *New Scientist* and *Scientific American*. It is designed to cater for the needs of secondary schools in Australia.
- AUSTHealth: a number of Australian health databases—APAIS Health: a subset of the APAIS database on health and medicine (excluding clinical medicine); AMI (Australasian Medical Index): Australian health and medical journals not covered by Medline; ABOR (Aboriginal and Torres Strait Islander Health Bibliography): material on Australian indigenous health status (excluding social and political factors).
- AustLII (Australasian Legal Information Institute): free web access to Australian legal material (legislation and decisions of courts and tribunals), including material produced by law reform and royal commission reports (http://www.austlii.edu.au).
- AEI (Australian Education Index): education and related fields.
- ALISA (Australian Library & Information Science Abstracts): Australian index on library and information services, technology and electronic publishing.
- ARCH (Australian Architecture Database): architects, landscape, building and interior design.
- ATI (Australian Tourism Index): tourism and travel index of publications.
- AUSPORT (Australian Sport Database): coaching, administration, disabilities, sport nutrition and sport psychology.
- Biological Abstracts: international life science journals covering

agriculture, biochemistry, biomedicine, biotechnology, botany, ecology, microbiology, pharmacology and zoology.

- CINAHL (Cumulative Index to Nursing and Allied Health Literature): an international database with good Australian and New Zealand coverage.
- CINCH: Australian criminology database on most aspects of crime, including crime prevention, criminal law, criminology, law enforcement and victims of crime.
- CONSUMER: a consumer science index of journal articles.
- Current Contents: contents pages and abstracts for over 7000 journals in the sciences, social sciences, arts and humanities. Database is updated weekly. Features include an automated alerting service for table of contents of specified journals and articles.
- EconLit: produced by the American Economic Association, it is the premiere international database in economics, including articles since 1969.
- ERIC (Educational Resources Information Center): sponsored by the US Department of Education, it is the largest education database in the world.
- Expanded Academic ASAP International: a bibliographic and full-text database for journals on the arts, humanities, social sciences and sciences since 1980. Updated weekly. A separate Health Reference Center–Academic database lists articles from 1994 onwards on fitness, nutrition, public health and medicine.
- FirstSearch: bibliographic and full-text databases in science, social sciences, humanities and life sciences. Includes specialised databases such as GEOREF (geography), GEOBASE (geography), INSPEC (physics), Electrical Engineering and Computing.
- FAMILY: produced by the Australian Institute of Family Studies (AIFS), it covers all aspects of Australian research, policy and practice on the family and related issues, such as youth, the aged, marriage, divorce, adoption, child abuse, child care and domestic violence.
- Film International: information on over 100 000 films and cinema personalities.
- LLBA (Linguistics Language & Behavior Abstracts): interdisciplinary index and abstracts of international literature on linguistics, language and communication.
- Literature On-line: a web-based database of over 300 000 works of English and American literature.
- Philosopher's Index: an international database of key journals.
- MathSciNet: a web-based database providing access to *Mathematical Reviews*, a monthly reference journal where professional mathematicians review current published research. Updated weekly.
- Medline: the premiere database for biomedical literature. Also

includes dental, nursing, allied health, humanities and information science as applied to medicine and health care. Free access can be gained from the National Library of Medicine web site (http://www.nlm.nih.gov).
- MLA Bibliography: produced by the Modern Language Association of America, it indexes journal articles, monographs and dissertations on literature, language, linguistics and folklore.
- PsycLit: the electronic version of Psychological Abstracts, the premiere psychology database.
- Science Citation Index/Social Science Citation Index: two indexes, one covering the physical and life sciences, the other the social sciences. You can search by title, author and particularly citation—that is, search for articles that have referenced a particular author or paper in their bibliography (a useful feature if you are looking for what others have written about a particular author or topic).
- Social Work Abstracts: international database of journal articles.
- Sociofile: the electronic version of Sociological Abstracts, the premiere resource for sociology and related disciplines.
- UnCover: an extensive, multi-disciplinary database of journal articles, journal contents pages and books. Features include the ability to order fax copies of the articles from the database, and an automated alerting service for table of contents of specified journals and articles selected by keywords (http://uncweb.carl.org).

Most electronic databases allow the use of Boolean operators. Other ways to limit a search are by date (to obtain information published in a specified period), by source (for example, for material appearing in specified journals) or by format (for example, only searching for video material). A number of indexes also allow the use of **proximity operators** (NEAR, NEXT), which search for keywords next to each other or near each other in a document. Most indexes also allow you to search for the exact phrase by placing your keywords in quotation marks, thereby ensuring an exact match (see HANDY HINT 6).

Searching for derivations of the same keyword: Using truncation

All on-line indexes allow the use of truncation symbols that let you search for words with the same root. For example:

Figure 4.1   A visual representation of Boolean operators at work

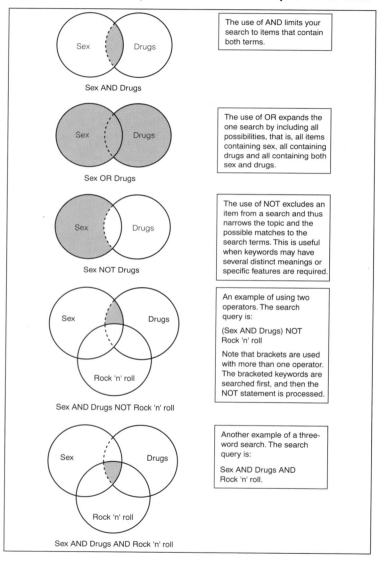

The use of AND limits your search to items that contain both terms.

Sex AND Drugs

The use of OR expands the one search by including all possibilities, that is, all items containing sex, all containing drugs and all containing both sex and drugs.

Sex OR Drugs

The use of NOT excludes an item from a search and thus narrows the topic and the possible matches to the search terms. This is useful when keywords may have several distinct meanings or specific features are required.

Sex NOT Drugs

An example of using two operators. The search query is:

(Sex AND Drugs) NOT Rock 'n' roll

Note that brackets are used with more than one operator. The bracketed keywords are searched first, and then the NOT statement is processed.

Sex AND Drugs NOT Rock 'n' roll

Another example of a three-word search. The search query is:

Sex AND Drugs AND Rock 'n' roll.

Sex AND Drugs AND Rock 'n' roll

- Enter sex★ and your search will include all words that begin with the same letters, such as sexual, sexuality, sexology, sexual dysfunction, sexism . . .

You can also use the truncation symbol to search for a word which may have a number of different spellings. For example:

- Enter organi★ation and this will cover all spellings of the word—in this case, organisation and organization.

As in the above example, the use of a truncation symbol is particularly useful to cover differences in spelling in American English. The actual symbol used varies according to the electronic database, but the most common symbols are: ★, ?, +, $ or #.

HANDY HINT 6: Boolean and other options

When using Boolean operators, most indexes use capitals to distinguish the words as commands—for example, women AND dieting. Some on-line indexes also provide check boxes or drop down menus that offer a choice of Boolean options (to save you typing them) along with other means to refine your search, such as by date or language, or by searching only for the keywords in the title of a work. These options can be particularly helpful to narrow the number of 'hits' you get.

An example of conducting a search using the Sociofile index

We searched the Sociofile database for the keywords: women AND dieting. We limited the search to articles published in English between 1996 and 1998. The search revealed five 'hits' that were displayed on our computer screen as shown in Figure 4.2.

As you can see from the figure, the Sociofile data-base, like many others, provides plenty of information. Full details of the author(s), article title and journal are given, along with the note that an abstract is available. Using your mouse to click on an entry provides further detailed information. For example, by clicking on entry five the following information was revealed on our screen as shown in Figure 4.3.

Note that the keywords are highlighted, indicating that Sociofile searches the abstract as well as the title of journal articles in its database. The extra information provided below the abstract can also be useful. For example, the words listed under 'Subject Headings' provide links to other articles on those topics. Therefore, by simply clicking on 'Body Image', Sociofile lists another 83 articles on that topic (using the original parameters of English-only articles published between 1996 and 1998).

Figure 4.2 Sociofile results

1 Hart, Kathleen; Kenny, Maureen E. Adherence to the Super Woman Ideal and Eating Disorder Symptoms among College Women. [Abstract of Journal Article] Sex Roles, 1997, 36, 7–8, Apr, 461–478.

2 Harrison, Kristen; Cantor, Joanne. The Relationship between Media Consumption and Eating Disorders. [Abstract of Journal Article] Journal of Communication, 1997, 47, 1, winter, 40–67.

3 Grogan, Sarah; Wainwright, Nicola. Growing Up in the Culture of Slenderness: Girls' Experiences of Body Dissatisfaction. [Abstract of Journal Article] Women's Studies International Forum, 1996, 19, 6, Nov–Dec, 665–673.

4 Fear, Jennifer L.; Bulik, Cynthia M.; Sullivan, Patrick F. The Prevalence of Disordered Eating Behaviours and Attitudes in Adolescent Girls. [Abstract of Journal Article] New Zealand Journal of Psychology, 1996, 25, 1, June, 7–12.

5 Germov, John; Williams, Lauren. The Sexual Division of Dieting: Women's Voices. [Abstract of Journal Article] Sociological Review, 1996, 44, 4, Nov, 630–647.

As you can see, electronic index and abstract databases can be an extremely useful and efficient way to search for information in journals. However, note that while on-line electronic databases offer many advantages over their printed versions, many indexes remain published only in hard-copy form. Also, many electronic databases do not contain the full listing of their printed versions—for example, very few indexes will include material from the 1970s or earlier, and in some cases the electronic form of the database only dates back to the 1980s. Therefore, do not discard the fact that you may still need to use the printed versions of index and abstract databases, even though your first 'port of call' should be the electronic versions.

Subject headings and on-line thesauri

All indexes have their own search hints, guidelines and/or help keys that you should consult. Many also have a thesaurus that lists keywords used to organise material in that particular index and abstract. The on-line thesaurus is

Figure 4.3   Sociofile results continued

Author
   Germov, John. Williams, Lauren.

Title
   The Sexual Division of **Dieting**: **Women**'s Voices.

Source
   Sociological Review, 1996, 44, 4, Nov, 630–647

Abstract
Focus group data collected 1994/95 from 14 **women** in Gosford &
Sydney, Australia, who have engaged in **dieting** practices to lose weight
indicate that (1) **women** participate in the perpetuation & reinforcement
of the thin ideal; (2) they clearly trade off health in the pursuit of
dieting to lose weight; & (3) the dominant discourse of the thin ideal is
not only mediated in various ways, but is also contested by a reverse
discourse of size acceptance. A sociology of food & the body enables
the discourses in the area of **dieting women** to be deconstructed,
offering an insight into the gendered context of food, which has
implications for the sociology of health & illness. 45 References.
Adapted from the source document.
(Copyright 1997, Sociological Abstracts, Inc., all rights reserved.)

Subject Headings
   *Body Weight
   *Diet
   *Discourse Analysis
   *Females
   *Food
   *Body Image
   *Australia

Classification Codes
   Sociology of health and medicine: sociology of medicine & health
   care (2045).

Language
   English.

Country of Publication
   United Kingdom.

Publication Type
   Abstract of Journal Article.

HANDY HINT 7: Getting access to on-line indexes

Most university libraries have placed index databases on the web to allow multiple user and 24-hour remote access to their journal databases. However, access to many university-based library databases may be restricted to students and staff of the university via passwords as part of a licensing agreement. Nonetheless, you might like to try to access some university and state or national library web sites (see the appendix).

a list of terms (sometimes called descriptors or subjects) most likely, but not exclusively, constructed from the Library of Congress Subject Headings (LCSH) and Medical Subject Headings (MESH) publications. The most common method of searching an electronic catalogue is via 'free-text' searching—that is, using any keywords you can think of to try and match sources of information in the database. However, if your search is unsuccessful or you need help coming up with keywords, check to see if an on-line or hard-copy thesaurus is available for the particular database you are using. This allows you to search for items by subject, irrespective of whether the actual word appears in the article. This can be helpful when authors use vague terms or if you are looking for highly specialised terms that are unlikely to appear in titles or even abstracts. For access to on-line indexes, see HANDY HINT 7.

Other sources of journal article information: Annual Review journals

A good place to look for overviews of specific topics are Annual Review journals which attempt to canvass the 'hot topics' for a particular year. These are obviously helpful,

Table 4.2   A sample of the Annual Review journals that are available

- *Annual Review of Applied Linguistics*
- *Annual Review of Astronomy and Astrophysics*
- *Annual Review of Biochemistry*
- *Annual Review of Genetics*
- *Annual Review of Nutrition*
- *Annual Review of Psychology*
- *Annual Review of Nursing Research*
- *Annual Review of Sex Research*
- *Annual Review of Sociology*

and the references cited by the relevant articles can also be used as a springboard to find further information. Annual Review journals exist for almost all disciplines, a sample of which are listed in Table 4.2.

Using the annual index of journals

Most journals publish an annual index of the contents of the journal in the last issue of the year. These are particularly worth seeking out for two main reasons:

- The most recent journal articles on a topic (in the current year) will not yet have been recorded in an indexed database.
- To determine if any **review articles** of key topics have been published. This is particularly common, but not exclusively so, in profession-based journals which tend regularly to publish 'state of the art' style articles on specific topics.

On-line e-journals

There is an increasing number of **e-journals** (electronic journals) being published. In addition, existing journal publishers are providing their hard-copy journals in electronic format as well. In most cases, e-journal web sites only contain the contents pages and abstracts of articles, while a few

HANDY HINT 8: Library search checklist

Chapters 3 and 4 have provided you with the knowledge and skills you will need to search for books, other material and journal articles. The following checklist summarises the main tips:

- Do a library tour to orientate yourself to the physical layout of your library, its on-line cataloguing system and the electronic databases it provides.
- Check to see if your library produces printed discipline-specific search help guides.
- Before using an electronic database, read the information guide for search tips.
- Consult the on-line thesaurus of keywords for a particular database.
- Always search a number of databases to ensure that you cover the field. If older material is relevant to your search, note the date from which the index you are using started to include material.
- Use Boolean and proximity operators to expand or narrow your keyword searches.
- Be aware of differences in US spelling and terminology.
- Use truncated symbols where necessary.
- If you are unsure or in doubt, ask a librarian for help.

actually provide the full text of their contents on the web. To find an e-journal relevant to your area, try the following web sites:

- The Internet Public Library on-line serials page: http://www.ipl.org/reading/serials
- E-journal directories: http://www.aph.gov.au/library/intguide/gen/genejrnl.htm
- NewJour: http://gort.ucsd.edu/newjour

Using inter-library loans to overcome the limits of your library

It is important to note that the sources you identify in indexes and abstract databases will not necessarily be available in your own library. Unlike the on-line library catalogues for book and journal titles which usually list only library holdings, electronic databases list all articles whether or not your library holds a copy of that actual journal. This can be disappointing, especially when you find a great article. However, you may still be able to get hold of the article. Most university libraries allow students access to inter-library loans—that is, they are able to borrow material from other libraries. However, requesting and transferring material from one library to another can take two or more weeks, so allow for this time delay in meeting your deadline. There may also be costs involved in the request, so choose your inter-library loan carefully. HANDY HINT 8 summarises the key strategies you need to search the library and on-line catalogues effectively.

The next chapter shows you how to search the web and find quality information.

5 The Internet I: Webbing it

- *What are the short cuts to finding relevant information on the web?*
- *How can you avoid 900 000 'hits' using a web search engine?*
- *How can you use the Internet to do research for you automatically?*

The Internet: A path through the cyberspace jungle

There has been so much hype about the 'information super-highway', 'surfing the Net' and 'cyberspace' that many people are confused, sceptical and even suspicious of what the Internet really has to offer. The word 'Internet' is an abbreviation of the words 'international network' and describes the ability of computers to exchange information, entertainment, commerce and public communication through the global telecommunications system. The Internet is made up of:

- the World Wide Web (WWW or the web)
- electronic mail (e-mail), **mailing lists** and **Usenet**

HANDY HINT 9: What are Gopher, FTP and Telnet?

The Internet actually existed before the web, with information archived and accessed on the Internet via a system called **Gopher**, which is based on a hierarchical organisation of information into parent directories and sub-directories. Since much effort went into establishing Gopher sites, many still exist and continue to be accessed on the Internet, but they are gradually being replaced by the more user-friendly web.

You may also come across the abbreviations 'FTP' and 'Telnet'. FTP stands for **'file transfer protocol'** and is simply a software program that allows you to transfer files electronically from one computer to another. **Telnet** (short for telecommunications network) is a software program that enables a computer to connect to another computer system to access databases at another location.

newsgroups, which are e-mail-based discussion forums (see Chapter 6)
- Gopher, FTP and Telnet (see HANDY HINT 9).

The web is by far the most common way of accessing information and therefore is the focus of this chapter. The popularity of the web is based on its capacity to overcome the tyranny of distance for communication and information exchange by providing access to all sorts of information at a keystroke and a mouse click from your desktop. The great advantage of the web over other aspects of the Internet is that it allows the transmission of multimedia information—text, graphics, animation, audio and video. The web is a wonderful resource tool and literally gives you global and immediate access to information. However, like all tools, there are a few 'tricks of the trade' you will need to know to use it effectively.

**Figure 5.1   The Netscape browser showing the LookSmart
web site**

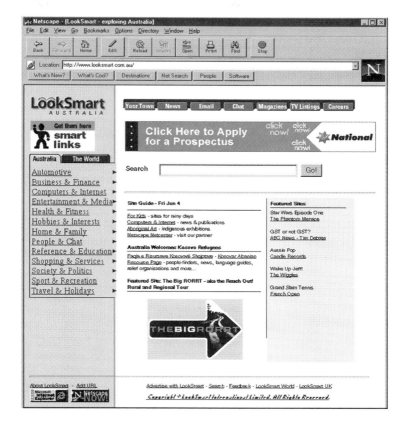

Web basics

The web is accessed via a software program known as a
browser. Netscape and Internet Explorer are examples of
web browser programs. An example of the Netscape browser
is shown in Figure 5.1.

Near the top of the Netscape browser is the 'Netsite',

HANDY HINT 10: What is a URL?
Making sense of web addresses

A URL (web address) is made up of a number of parts. To understand the components of a URL, let's look at the following address for one of our other books

http://www.newcastle.edu.au/department/so/socialappetite.htm

and see what it means:

- **http**: refers to hyper-text transfer protocol (the computer language used to access the web). Note that the newer versions of web browsers automatically include the 'http' part of a URL when they search for a web address, saving you the trouble of having to type 'http' every time you enter a different URL.
- **www**: is an abbreviation for World Wide Web. This part of the web address refers to the name of the actual computer where the web site is located in a particular organisation. Many organisations commonly name their web computer 'www'.
- **newcastle.edu.au**: this part of the web address refers to the actual location of the web page at a particular organisation. The word 'newcastle' refers to the name of the organisation, followed by 'edu' which is an abbreviation for educational institution, followed by 'au', the country of origin code (which in this case is Australia).
- **department/so/socialappetite**: the last section of a URL is the directory, sub-directory and filename of the document displayed on the screen. Our address indicates that the document 'socialappetite.htm' is located in the sub-directory 'so' (which in this case stands for sociology), which is in the directory 'department'.
- **htm**: refers to hyper-text markup language (sometimes the abbreviation 'html' is used), which is a computer language used to write web pages.

URL abbreviations
All URLs use abbreviations to indicate the type of organisation and the country where the web site is located. Common organisation abbreviations include:

- edu: educational (ac for academic in the UK)
- com: commercial organisation (co in the UK)
- net: Internet access provider
- gov: government agency
- org: non-government/non-profit organisation.

Most, but not all, addresses will include a country code, except for the United States. It is fairly safe to assume that if a URL has no country code, then the site is probably located in the United States. Some examples of country codes are:

- ca: Canada
- de: Germany
- jp: Japan
- nz: New Zealand
- uk: United Kingdom.

or location box, in which you enter a web address. A web address is much like a postal address and tells your browser where to search the Internet to locate a particular web site. A web address is known as a **Uniform Resource Locator (URL)** (pronounced 'you-are-ell'). (See HANDY HINT 10 for further explanation.)

Connecting to a web site

There are four basic ways to find a web site:

1 If you know the URL, just type it into the browser location box and press enter.
2 When you don't know the web address, you can make a guess as to the likely web address (see HANDY HINT 11).

HANDY HINT 11: Guessing a web address

Many well-known organisations incorporate their name into their web address, making it easy to find their web sites. If you know the name of the organisation you are looking for, try guessing the actual web address. While there is no guarantee that you will get it right, sometimes trying a 'literal' web address can save you time. Here are a few obvious examples:

- IBM: http://www.ibm.com
- Toyota: http://www.toyota.com
- Netscape: http://www.netscape.com

3   If your guess fails, you can use a web search engine or subject directory to find specific web site URLs (which this chapter shows you how to do).
4   Another method of moving from one web page to another is by clicking on a **hyper-text** link, from a gateway or specialist web site (described below).

Web pages often contain hyper-text links—which are indicated by different coloured text, underlined text or highlighted graphics. Hyper-text links are pre-programmed web addresses that allow you to roam around the web in an easy, non-linear way. The great advantage of hyper-text links is that you can jump from one web site to another by a click of your mouse button, without having to type in the web address (URL) yourself. For example, Figure 5.2 shows a web page with a table of hyper-text links to various book publishers. You can position your cursor over the highlighted words 'Allen & Unwin'—a hyper-text link—and by clicking your mouse button you are automatically taken to the web site for Allen & Unwin, an independent Australian book publisher.

In whatever way you get to a web address, the first

Figure 5.2   Using a hyper-text link on a web page

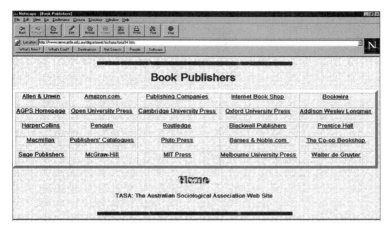

screen you see displayed when your browser retrieves information from a web site is called the **home page** of that
site. From there you can click on links to move to other
'pages' within the site. If you need further help in understanding how to use a web browser, we encourage you to
make use of the many 'how to' books and short courses that
are widely available.

Searching the web: Search engines, subject directories and meta-indexes

Even though the number of web sites grows daily, there are
thankfully a number of catalogue and indexing services
available that make searching the web a lot easier. Search
engines, subject directories and meta-indexes are information
retrieval systems. These facilities are used in a similar fashion
to on-line library catalogues, but are accessed via the web.
Once you have determined your specific keywords (see
Chapter 2 for help with this), you simply enter them into the

Figure 5.3   An example of the Excite search engine

web index like you would a library catalogue. However, you should be aware of a big misconception about web search engines, directories and indexes—they do not search the entire web when you enter a keyword search request. What they actually do is search their own massive databases of sites they have indexed. Therefore, web catalogues are never complete and it is often wise to use a few different ones to ensure a thorough search. Furthermore, because the web is such a dynamic entity, thousands of new sites are established daily, while many others cease to exist. The following sections explain how to use three different types of web catalogue.

Search engines

A search engine is a catalogue of web sites that can be searched by keyword queries (see Figure 5.3 for a sample web page).

Table 5.1 **Comparing search engine results**

Keywords	Excite results	InfoSeek results
occupational health and safety (entire web)	2 643 591	7 329 848
'occupational health and safety' (entire web)	11 970	22 116
'occupational health and safety' (Australia only)	1 001	253
occupational AND health AND safety (Australia only)	240	16

Search engine catalogues are compiled by computer programs that automatically search the web and index the web sites found. Search engines provide by far the largest database in which to perform keyword searches for relevant web sites, even though they are not totally comprehensive due to the limitations mentioned previously.

If you have more than one keyword, a search engine does not automatically look for a relationship between the words, only that they both appear somewhere in the text of the web pages it has indexed. However, all search engines offer 'advanced search' options which are often based on Boolean and proximity operators (explained in Chapter 4). These options allow you to limit your search for exact matches to phrases, or even to phrases that only occur in the title of a web page. You can even search for web sites in specific countries and regions (such as the United Kingdom or Oceania).

What does a web search look like?

Table 5.1 provides an example of search engine results of a keyword search for the topic 'occupational health and safety', using a number of options and comparing the results from the Excite and InfoSeek search engines. As you can see from the example, each search engine returns a different number of keyword 'hits', even for the advanced search options. This example shows the importance of using a number of search engines and advanced options. (Note the use of the Boolean operator AND in the last query.)

Most search engines also rank keyword matches for relevance, usually as a percentage score, listing the retrieved sites in descending order of relevance. Therefore, the first ten or twenty 'hits' are most likely to have what you are looking for if you've been successful in refining your search parameters. However, these rankings should be treated as a basic guide only. They are usually determined by a couple of simple criteria, such as whether the keywords you entered occur in the title of the web page and the frequency of the keywords in the web page. They do not indicate the quality of the web site.

Search engine golden rules

When using any search engine, the golden rules to follow for getting the best results are:

- Use more than one keyword.
- Always use the advanced search options (Boolean and proximity operators).
- Always read the search tips of the particular search engine you use. (Slight differences exist between them.)
- Place keywords in quotation marks (if the search engine allows this) so that the words are searched for as a phrase. (That is, the keywords must all be next to each other.)
- **Bookmark** the web sites you find useful for future visits. All browsers have a bookmark facility that allows you to simply record a web address after which you can check your bookmarks file and click on the entry which acts like a hyper-text link and takes you automatically to the web page without having to remember and type in the actual URL.

There are many search engines available to choose from. We recommend the following ones for their coverage and consistency in producing reliable results:

- Altavista: http://www.altavista.com
- Excite: http://www.excite.com
- Hotbot: http://www.hotbot.com
- InfoSeek: http://www.infoseek.com
- LookSmart: http://www.looksmart.com.au

You will note from the lack of a country designation in the above search engine web addresses that they are all located in the United States. Since most of the search engines are based in the United States they don't have extensive coverage of web sites elsewhere—this is where the local versions of search engines can be valuable (see HANDY HINT 12).

If you are interested in a comparison of the performance of the search engines that are available, the following two web sites provide an up-to-date list of search engines and their performance:

- Search Engine Watch:
  http://www.searchenginewatch.com
- W3 Search Engines:
  http://osiris.sunderland.ac.uk/rif/W3searches.htm

If you are having trouble getting through to a web site, or it seems particularly slow, you might like to visit the Internet Traffic Report:

- Internet Traffic Report:
  http://www.internettrafficreport.com

This web site provides a rating on the flow of data around the world. The rating is given as a value between 0 and 100, with higher ratings indicating a faster connection. For example, when we visited the site, the rating for Australia was 56, compared to 42 for Europe and 53 for Asia. Therefore, the connection times were slowest in Europe, indicating more Internet traffic in the region. You can find more information on a particular country by clicking on a region.

Subject directories

Subject directories have much smaller databases than search engines and therefore you are less likely to suffer the problem of information overload. As noted above, search engines use computer programs to find and index web sites automatically, which can lead to problems such as poor-quality and poorly indexed sites. Directories, on the other hand, overcome this problem because they are compiled by people who categorise web sites into subject categories in much the same way as librarians catalogue books. Web directories provide a large range of subject categories and tend to organise their content in a hierarchy of ever-diminishing sub-directories. Because people have done the categorisation, subject directories can help to narrow your web search, but are not as comprehensive as search engines. We recommend the following subject directories:

* Yahoo: http://www.yahoo.com.au
* InfoPlease: http://www.Infoplease.com
* InfoSeek Guide: http://www.infoseek.com
* Lycos: http://www.lycos.com
* Magellan: http://www.mckinley.com
* Suite101: http://www.suite101.com
* WWW Virtual Library: http://www.w3.org/vl

The distinction between search engines and subject directories is blurring, as engines increasingly catalogue their web pages into subject categories and directories to improve the search facilities of their databases. The best advice to follow is to use both. Perhaps start with a subject directory if you have a clear idea of the keywords for the topic you are after. You can then use a search engine to search for further web sites. Since search engines and directories find and catalogue web sites in slightly different ways, it is always best to use a number of them to ensure maximum coverage. Eventually, you will probably find a couple of engines and directories that you prefer and end up using them regularly. There are also local or regional

HANDY HINT 12: Local versions of engines and directories

Many of the major search engines and subject directories have established local or regional versions, such as Yahoo Australia: http://www.yahoo.com.au. Those that have not done so may allow you to specify a country in your search. Our current favourite is LookSmart for its coverage and ease of use, but there are a number of other Australian indexes worth consulting:

- LookSmart: http://www.looksmart.com.au (see Figure 5.3)
- WebWombat: http://www.webwombat.com.au
- Anzwers: http://www.anzwers.com.au
- Aussie Index: http://www.aussie.com.au/index
- OzSearch: http://www.ozsearch.com.au
- This is Australia:
  http://springboard.telstra.com.au/index.html
- Excite Australia: http://au.excite.com

versions of some of the well-known search engines and directories (see HANDY HINT 12).

A highly recommended and easy to navigate subject directory is the Encyclopaedia Britannica Internet Guide:

- http://www.eblast.com

The staff of Encyclopaedia Britannica have classified, rated and reviewed high-quality web sites, providing annotated descriptions of each web site and statistics on site speed and usage rates.

An increasingly popular site is Ask Jeeves, because it allows you to enter a search request using plain English. For example, you could Ask Jeeves the questions: 'Why is the earth round?' or 'How far is the moon from the earth?' There is no need for Boolean operators here and hence it is very user-friendly.

- Ask Jeeves: http://www.askjeeves.com

HANDY HINT 13: Troubleshooting tips for when web addresses fail

It is not uncommon to attempt to connect to a web site only to receive an error message. There are several possible reasons for this:

* Web addresses change and some disappear altogether. This will be true of some of the addresses given in this chapter as the book ages, although we will continue to update them on the *Get Great Information Fast* web page to avoid this problem.
* Human error.
* Computer glitches.

If an address you have entered fails, check the spelling by trying US spelling and checking the placement of full stops in the URL. Also, URLs never contain blank spaces, so watch out for these. Computer glitches are the other main reason, either because of too much Internet traffic or network problems at the destination. If an address doesn't reach its destination, always try to resend it—it will often get through on the second try. It is also not uncommon for the computer server at a particular organisation to be under repair, so if you are sure the address is correct and keep getting an error message, always try the address again in a day or so. Sometimes, the software glitch may be at your end and you might have to log off and on again.

If the web address is obviously incorrect or has changed, there are two things you can do:

1 Search for the web page through a search engine by putting in the key parts of the original web address.
2 Gradually delete parts of the web address you have by working from right to left, deleting a part of the address and then trying to see if you get a connection with the remainder of the address. Eventually you will get to the generic host home page, from which you may be able

> to deduce if the web site exists. For example, let's say
> the original address below no longer works:
> http://www.newcastle.edu.au/department/so/socialappetite.htm
> Try:
> http://www.newcastle.edu.au/department/so/socialappetite
> And if that doesn't work, try:
> http://www.newcastle.edu.au/department/so
> And if it still doesn't work then try:
> http://www.newcastle.edu.au/department
>
> Once you get back to the first part of the address—
> www.newcastle.edu.au—you will not be able to strip back
> the URL any further. If you still have no luck, then some-
> times you have to accept that web sites simply vanish into
> the virtual air of cyberspace.

Meta-indexes and 'all-in-one' search sites

'All-in-One' or multi-access sites provide a list of various
search engines that can be accessed via the one web page.
This has the advantage of using a variety of search engines
without having to visit their individual web sites and know
their individual URLs. The drawback of using such multiple
access search sites is that they generally only allow a basic
keyword search, meaning that advanced search options are
unavailable. Examples of such sites include:

- All-in-One: http://www.albany.net.allinone
- W3 Search Engines:
  http://osiris.sunderland.ac.uk/rif/w3searches.html
- Internet Sleuth: http://www.isleuth.com
- Webtaxi: http://www.webtaxi.com

  A highly recommended search site is:

- CNet Search.com: http://www.search.cnet.com

This web site is a combination all-in-one search engine site and subject directory. You can access a number of search engines that either cover the whole web or specialise in specific areas. The specialist sites comprise other search engines, archives and indexes on selected topics, including classifieds, computing, employment, entertainment, health, learning, news and travel, to name a few. By choosing a topic, you are presented with a preferred search engine/archive, or you can scroll through the A–Z list and choose your own. This is an easy to navigate and extensive site that would make a good starting-point for any search.

Meta-indexes allow you to conduct keyword searches using a number of different search engines at the one time. A meta-index provides one search form interface where you enter your keywords. These are then posted to a number of search engines, with the findings combined in one list of results. Such a method is likely to provide a high number of 'hits' and can be useful to gain an understanding of the range of information available on a topic. However, advanced search options are unavailable and therefore you are likely to have many irrelevant hits to your search queries. The most common meta-indexes are:

- Dogpile: http://www.dogpile.com
- Inference Find: http://www.inference.com/ifind
- Internet Sleuth: http://www.isleuth.com
- MetaCrawler: http://www.metacrawler.com
- Metafind: http://www.metafind.com
- SavvySearch: http://guaraldi.cs.colostate.edu:2000

Multiple browsing

One final time-saving method of searching the web is via multiple browsing. Internet traffic and the large size of some web sites mean that it can take time to reach and access certain sites. To save time, you can multi-task by running a number of web sessions at the one time. Just as in Windows, where you can run a number of programs simultaneously, you can conduct multiple searches of the web by clicking on the 'File' drop down menu of your browser and choosing 'New Browser' or 'New Window'. This opens up another browser, so that you can have more than one operating at the same time during which you can search for different web sites. This can be particularly helpful when you are downloading a large document from the web which can often be time-consuming. However, the catch is that the time saved will depend on your computer's memory and speed. The more pressure placed on your computer's resources, the greater the chance it may 'freeze' or 'crash'. Sometimes a web site will automatically open a new window for you when you access a special feature, particularly when browsing and downloading large documents and files. When this happens, your 'back' button becomes inoperable and you need to close the new window to go back to the previous page. Alternatively, you can press the 'alt' and 'tab' keys on your keyboard simultaneously to move between the previous and the current web page.

Web short-cuts: Using specialist sites

The best advice to save time in searching the web is to locate specialist sites compiled by individuals and organisations that have already done the hard work for you and established subject directories on virtually every topic imaginable. Specialist web sites worth consulting regularly include:

- government web sites
- university web sites
- national and state library web sites
- web rings
- clearinghouses, gateways and virtual libraries.

Below we list a number of key web sites at which you should find links to all of your information needs.

Government

Many government organisations provide web directories of subject-oriented links. For example, in Australia the Parliamentary Library of Australia web site is one of the best web resources in the country.

- http://www.aph.gov.au/library

This site includes links on social policy issues, all media outlets, politics and administration, law, science and technology, statistics and other Internet resources. Specific resources provided include:

- *Hansard*: the transcript of parliamentary debates of the Australian federal government. The House of Representatives' Hansard is called *Votes and Proceedings*; the Senate Hansard is called *Journals of the Senate*. The records of state parliaments have various names, such as *Minutes* or *Proceedings* (links to all state governments can be found at this site).
- *Parliamentary Papers*: a series of reports tabled in the federal Parliament, such as departmental annual reports, policy discussion papers and reports of royal commissions.
- *What's New*: the parliamentary library produces a weekly listing of key books, reports, articles and transcripts received in the library. This service includes transcripts of important TV and radio interviews and programs, such as 'Four Corners' (ABC TV in Australia).
- All media releases from parliamentarians.
- Information on political parties, individual parliamentarians and election results.
- A range of material on social policy issues and background briefings on current 'hot' political topics are also available.

Governments produce many documents and reports that contain valuable information, many of which are increasingly available on government web pages.

* Australian government: http://www.fed.gov.au
* Governments of the world: http://www.hg.org/govt.html

For information on new legislation and court decisions, try:

* Attorney-General's Department web site: http://law.gov.au/
* Australasian Legal Information Institute: http://www.austlii.edu.au/
* Australian Law Reform Commission: http://www.alrc.gov.au
* International law links: http://www.aph.gov.au/library/intguide/law

Universities

You can save yourself a great deal of research time on the web by accessing various university web sites. By now, most university academic disciplines will have their own web sites which will often have a 'hotlinks' section. These discipline web links are great time-savers. Another trick is to visit the university library web site. It is increasingly common that librarians are developing specialist subject-oriented web sites as well. Key university web site links are listed below:

* Australian universities: http://www.mc.com.au/index.html
* Australian university library web sites: http://www.anu.edu.au/caul/uni-libs.htm
* Universities (world): http://www.mit.edu:8001/people/cdemello/univ.html

In general, most aspects of a university's library web site will be open to public access, but, as noted in Chapter 4, access to some on-line search indexes may be restricted to staff and students of the university through a password, due to licensing agreements.

National and state libraries

One of the greatest information resources of any country is its national and state or regional libraries, most of which have a web presence. The following list of web links should allow you to find the library that best suits your needs:

- Australian Libraries Gateway: http://enzo.nla.gov.au/products/alg
- National Library of Australia: http://www.nla.gov.au
- National Libraries of the World: http://www.ifla.org/II/natlibs.htm
- The Electronic Library: http://www.books.com/scripts/lib.exe
- Librarians' Index to the Internet: http://sunsite.berkeley.edu/internetindex

Web rings

Web rings are lists of web sites that share the same subject area. As the name suggests, you enter the web ring and can then pursue related web sites that have joined the ring. Web rings exist for virtually every topic and are useful starting-points to find professional organisations that have established web sites of relevant and credible links on their subject or discipline area. However, there is no guarantee of quality, as just about anyone can link their web site to a ring if it matches the subject area.

- Web ring home page: http://www.webring.org

Clearinghouses, gateways and virtual libraries

There are an increasing number of web sites that provide useful lists of subject-specific links to other sites. Such web sites are often referred to as clearinghouses, gateways or virtual libraries, and are compiled by university academics and professional organisations and are therefore usually of high quality in terms of providing reliable information. For

HANDY HINT 14: Keep a web time-log

No matter how diligent you are in refining your web searches, you will invariably find yourself going off on a tangent. You will undoubtedly come across interesting, but irrelevant, web sites during your information quest. Try not to let your inquisitiveness get the better of you. To minimise time-wastage and possible expense, keep a log of the time spent doing research on the web. This may help put things into perspective. If you do come across an interesting web site that is irrelevant to your current information needs, bookmark it and return to it when you have the time.

example, The Scout Report provides a very useful update service:

- The Scout Report:
  http://scout.cs.wisc.edu/scout/report/index.html

The Scout Report provides a brief annotated list of new and useful information resources on the Internet. It is published once a week and is available on the web or by e-mail. Previous reports are archived at the web site. You can also subscribe to or visit reports on three specialty areas: business and economics, science and engineering, and social sciences.

The most commonly used gateways are:

- The Argus Clearinghouse: http://www.clearinghouse.net
- The Internet Public Library: http://www.ipl.org
- SOSIG: Social Science Information Gateway:
  http://sosig.ac.uk/welcome.html
- Suite101: http://www.suite101.com
- WWW Virtual Library: http://www.w3.org/vl

Keeping up to date: Auto-pilot research via push technology

The latest trend in information technology is 'push technology', where you subscribe to a service, sometimes for a small fee, to be sent information automatically at regular intervals via e-mail. For example, the journal article index databases Uncover and Current Contents will send you weekly updates of new books, articles and journal contents for the journals and subject areas you have specified. In this way you automatically keep up to date with publication areas that interest you. For example, on 10 August 1999, the Uncover database automatically delivered to our e-mail address five articles that matched the keyword 'best-practice'. In this case, we receive a weekly e-mail update for each keyword we have requested. We can also nominate journals that the database covers and receive the latest contents page. As can be expected, for some weeks there are no matches and no one database provides comprehensive coverage.

Push technology is commonly used for the free delivery of news, sports and weather information. Some specific newspapers such as the *Australian* offer this service, or you can go to a multi-source provider, such as PointCast or NewsTracker, that offers selected news from sources such as Reuters, Cable News Network, the *Wall Street Journal*, the *New York Times* and Australian news sources. Such services allow you to tailor the information you receive from the sources you want. Push technology is a clear example of the great advantage of the Internet. Key providers of news push technology are:

- PointCast: http://www.pointcast.com
- Downtown: http://www.incommon.com
- Netscape In-Box Direct: http://www.netscape.com.au
- NewsTracker: http://www.excite.com
- The Australian: http://www.theaustralian.com.au

- ABC News: http://www.abc.net.au/news
- Yahoo! International News Headlines:
  http://www.dailynews.yahoo.com/headlines

Journal publishers are establishing web sites for many of their journals. By visiting the journal web site, you may be able to subscribe to a contents-update e-mail service. A comprehensive list of electronic journals is available at NewJour:

- http://gort.ucsd.edu/newjour

A further method of keeping up to date automatically is by joining a mailing list relevant to your area of interest (see Chapter 6).

Keeping your finger on the pulse of web developments

Since the Internet is now a fact of life, we encourage you to keep up to date with web developments by regularly using one of the many Internet guides available. Our favourites are listed below:

- The Rough Guide to the Internet:
  http://www.roughguides.com/net
  The Rough Guide to the Internet is a pocket-size book full of easy to understand information. It's inexpensive and comes with its own web site full of interesting and entertaining links.
- The Internet Tourbus: http://www.tourbus.com
  The Internet Tourbus is an ongoing free guide to the Internet. You join the mailing list and receive a twice-weekly posting of handy hints, interesting web sites and myth-debunking. You can subscribe to the Tourbus at the web site, or simply visit it regularly and use its searchable archive. Highly recommended and the first

stop for finding an answer to your Internet query or problem.

The following Internet magazines, available in both hard-copy and web versions, are comprehensive, user-friendly and highly recommended for keeping up to date with what the web has to offer:
* NetGuide Magazine: http://www.netguide.com/home
* Hot Wired: http://www.hotwired.com
* Most capital city and national newspapers publish an information technology (IT) section or supplement, such as the *Weekend Australian* newspaper supplement, 'IT Living', which has its own web site: http://www.theaustralian.com.au

There are also many books that provide plenty of useful subject-specific web sites, e-mail discussion lists and news-groups. Look for the most recent editions, as the Internet is a dynamic area and such information can date quickly. You can also consult some of the introductory guides available on the web:

* Internet Beginners' Guide: http://www.blpes.lse.ac.uk/internet/beginners
* SOSIG Guide to the Internet: http://www.blpes.lse.ac.uk/internet
* World Wide Web FAQ: http://www.boutell.com.faq

Evaluating web information

You should always be cautious when you access information from the web. The reason for this is that anyone can place just about anything on the web—meaning that there is plenty of inaccurate 'info-trash' out there. A brief summary of the advantages and disadvantages of using the web as a source of information is provided in Table 5.2.

In terms of evaluating information obtained from the

Table 5.2   Web information: Advantages and disadvantages

Advantages	Disadvantages
Access to the latest information	Inconsistent indexing of information
Overcome physical, geographic and resource barriers	Lack of independent review of information
Encyclopaedic coverage	Continual changes to web sites and information
	Information overload

web, you should exercise the same caution as when determining the credibility of any information source. The key thing to remember is that some of the information you access may not have been independently checked before being published on the web and may therefore be unreliable. HANDY HINT 15 provides a quick web page evaluation checklist to ensure that the information you get from web pages is accurate and reliable.

The criteria for evaluating any information source are discussed further in Chapter 8. For a detailed discussion of critical evaluation skills for the web, you can access the training module on web evaluation by Jan Alexander and Marsha Tate:

• http://www.science.widener.edu/~withers/webeval.htm

Future developments

The old saying, 'the only constant is change', applies perfectly to the web. Changes and innovations are occurring rapidly. For example, as we go to press, a number of web search engines and subject directories are experimenting with 'clever' retrieval programs that rank matching sites to your search request according to ones that are most often clicked on or linked to by web users. Another major development in the foreseeable future is the expansion of information and entertainment delivery. For example, through on-line libraries

HANDY HINT 15: A checklist for evaluating web-based information

The key question to ask yourself when deciding to use information derived from a web site is: How can I tell if the information is accurate, up to date and comprehensive? The following checklist should help with the answer:

- Is web authorship of the information clearly identified?
- Is a publication date for the material given?
- Is contact information for the author/publisher provided?
- Can you trust the source of the information? For example, is the site produced by a special interest group, political party, commercial organisation, government body or educational institution? How might this affect the credibility and quality of the information presented?
- If the web site provides the results of academic research, is the work properly referenced? Is the methodology clearly stated (where relevant)? Has the work been independently peer-reviewed (such as in an academic journal)?
- The final point to remember is never to rely solely on one source of information—check print-based sources and other web sites on similar topics to confirm whether they support the information, findings and conclusions provided on the web site you have found.

you will be able, for a fee, to download books, movies, music and games to your desktop or hand-held personal computer. One final development gaining momentum is the use of web conferencing—the real-time exchange of messages posted on the web between a group of people, such as students in a distance-learning course. We are still in the early stages of

---

HANDY HINT 16: *Get Great Information Fast*
reader bonus

We would like to remind you that the appendix at the back
of this book lists key web sites by subject to help your
information search, all of which can be accessed via the
Get Great Information Fast web page:
http://www.allen-unwin.com.au/study/infofast.htm

---

the information revolution. Any further predictions we leave
to your imagination.

*Now that you have the web basics, the next chapter shows you
how to use e-mail to find information.*

6 The Internet II: E-mail, mailing lists and Usenet newsgroups

- *What are mailing lists and Usenet newsgroups and how can they be found?*
- *How can you use the Internet to find phone numbers and e-mail addresses?*
- *What are e-mail urban legends and what is netiquette?*

As mentioned previously, the Internet is not only the web but is also comprised of electronic mail (e-mail), now a major form of written communication that is likely to largely replace hard-copy letters (snail mail) and faxes. E-mails can be sent to individuals or discussion groups such as mailing lists and Usenet newsgroups to exchange information based on professional interests or hobbies. In this chapter we show you how to find relevant discussion lists and groups and introduce you to the basics of **netiquette** (Internet etiquette). While there are many e-mail discussion forums, the two major types are mailing lists and Usenet newsgroups.

Mailing lists

Mailing lists are a form of group e-mail which involves messages being sent simultaneously to all the people who have subscribed

HANDY HINT 17: Keep your confirmation message

When you join a mailing list, you will receive an automatic confirmation e-mail that welcomes you to the list and contains the basic instructions for sending messages and unsubscribing from the list. Always file these instructions in a separate mailing list folder, as you never know when you may need to use them. This is particularly helpful when you realise you have joined an inappropriate mailing list and you want to unsubscribe.

to the list. There are two types of mailing list: closed and open. Closed lists send information one way; you can receive a message, but you cannot contribute to the list. Closed lists are generally used to distribute information on a regular basis on a particular topic, and range from weather forecasts to this week's TV programs or the main headlines of today's news. Open lists involve two-way communication among all the subscribers to the list by allowing you to send an e-mail to the list that is then forwarded on to all the subscribers. Open lists can be moderated or unmoderated. Moderated lists have a list administrator who screens all the messages sent to it and deletes inappropriate or duplicated messages, thereby improving the quality of the messages. Since this takes time, unmoderated lists are most common and involve the automatic redistribution of a message to all the list subscribers. Some lists operate a weekly digest, where all the messages for the week are collated and sent in one e-mail, rather than separately. Once you subscribe to a list, you are automatically sent a confirmation message with further information about the list (see HANDY HINT 17). To find a mailing list to suit your interests, visit the following mailing list directories:

- Liszt: http://www.liszt.com
- Publicly Accessible Mailing Lists:
  http://www.neosoft.com/internet/palm

- Search the Net: http://www.statsvet.uu.se/maillist.html
- Reference.com: http://www.reference.com

Another way to find relevant lists is to ask the lecturers in your field which ones they subscribe to.

Newsgroups

Unlike a mailing list, you don't join a Usenet newsgroup or have messages delivered to your e-mail address. Rather, you visit a newsgroup—which is a location where you can post and read messages from anyone. Newsgroups are like bulletin boards, where anyone can post a message and anyone can read it if they choose. Therefore, you never know who or how many people may be reading your messages. Messages are grouped into topics called newsgroups and there are thousands of groups to choose from. You simply scan the newsgroups, find one that interests you, and either just passively read the messages others have posted or contribute yourself. While such groups can be useful forums for exchanging views, they are generally the least valuable or reliable source of information on the Internet and therefore we do not cover them in detail here. Our one tip is to always consult the **Frequently Asked Questions (FAQ)** file, which describes what the newsgroup is about, explains how to post messages and provides answers to common questions. Most newsgroups also compile a number of FAQs on subjects that have attracted a lot of interest. Therefore, to avoid sending a query or message that has long ago been covered by the newsgroup, always scan the FAQs for that group first. The following web sites provide a searchable database of Usenet newsgroups:

- DejaNews: http://www.dejanews.com
- Liszt Usenet Search: http://www.liszt.com

Finding people through the Internet: Phone and e-mail directories

Telephone white and yellow pages can be accessed via the web for many countries. To find the directory for various countries, visit:

* Telstra Springboard:
  http://www.springboard.telstra.com.au/directories/global.htm
* Telstra White Pages: http://www.whitepages.com.au
* Telstra Yellow Pages: http://www.yellowpages.com.au

There are a number of effective ways to find a person's e-mail address:

* If you know where they work, search for the web address of their organisation. Most organisations provide contact details of their employees through a staff directory.
* If you can't find it any other way and you have their phone number, call them and ask for their e-mail address.

If these two options fail, you can try one of a number of e-mail directories, such as:

* Bigfoot: http://www.bigfoot.com
* Four 11: http://www.four11.com
* Internet Address Finder: http://www.iaf.net
* WhoWhere?: http://www.whowhere.com
* Yahoo People: http://www.yahoo.com.au/search/people

Please note that these directories remain notoriously incomplete. For a good test of their scope, search for your own e-mail address and see if it comes up.

E-mail urban legends

An urban legend is a modern myth, usually a fantastic story that bears the hallmarks of credibility and has been popularised to such an extent that the sheer number of people that have heard about it lend it further credibility. E-mail urban legends abound and the most common of these is the friendly 'Virus alert' message warning you that a certain e-mail going around the Internet contains a virus that will do awful things to your computer. These messages are mostly written in alarmist language and are all hoaxes. They are generally passed on by unsuspecting e-mail users to friends and colleagues. There is *no* such thing as an e-mail virus. Whenever you receive such an e-mail, do not forward it on; instead, return it to the sender and inform them of the hoax. The only way you can get a computer virus from the Internet is by downloading a file from a web site or by opening a file that is attached to an e-mail. If you receive an unsolicited e-mail with a file attachment, it is preferable not to open it. Before you open any e-mail attachment, it is always good practice to scan the file with your virus checker. If you are interested in hoaxes on the Internet and other urban legends, you can visit the following web sites which index and debunk such hoaxes—and make for amusing reading:

• Urban legends:
  http://urbanlegends.miningco.com/library/blhoax.htm
• Computer virus myths: http://www.kumite.com/myths

Know your netiquette

Internet etiquette is quite simple: don't do anything you wouldn't want someone to do to you. Always remember that the Internet is a public domain, so behave as you normally would in any public space. The first rule is to generally avoid the use of CAPITALS in your e-mails—this makes the e-mail difficult to read and is often 'read' as anger or SHOUTING. Some other rules to know are:

• Always check the FAQ (Frequently Asked Questions) file of a Usenet newsgroup before posting a question to the group.

- Similarly, always keep the welcome/confirmation file sent to you when you first join a mailing list that contains information on how to unsubscribe from the list. Nothing annoys people on a list more than e-mails sent to the whole list asking how to unsubscribe.
- Never send personal e-mails that are directed at one person to a whole mailing list.
- Avoid sending unnecessary responses, such as 'I agree', 'Hear, hear', etc., to a mailing list—most people are already inundated by e-mails as it is.
- Avoid making defamatory remarks as a rule, particularly as it is quite easy to mistakenly send an e-mail to the wrong address! Furthermore, many employers are increasingly monitoring use of the Internet, particularly e-mails, so never assume that an e-mail is private and confidential. It's always good practice to be cautious when writing an e-mail—it could be on-line for a long time and forwarded all over the Internet.
- Never take part in flaming and spamming. Flaming refers to sending abusive e-mail messages to a particular address. Spamming refers to unsolicited e-mail that usually involves the selling of a product or service. Spamming is a 'fact of life' of the Internet and, while you can purchase various 'spam-buster' programs which are far from foolproof, spam e-mails are usually easy to identify so that you can immediately delete them from your e-mail in-box.
- Always include your name and your e-mail address so you can be contacted directly.
- Don't ask questions that you could easily find answers to yourself, and always stick to the topic of the news-group.

The language of the Net: Acronyms, smileys and emoticons

Computer jargon, particularly to do with the Internet, is usually the province of nerds and geeks with too much time

---

**HANDY HINT 18: Common Internet acronyms
and smileys**

Acronyms   **Smileys**
BFN: Bye for now   :-) Smiling
BTW: By the way   :-(Frowning
GAL: Get a life   :-D Laughing
HTH: Hope this helps   X-) I see nothing
LOL: Laughing out loud

---

on their hands. Net acronyms are common among Usenet newsgroups, but you may also find them in e-mails you receive. Smileys or emoticons are little symbols used to express sentiments or feelings. You don't need to remember them, but we provide a short list of the common acronyms and smileys that you may come across (see HANDY HINT 18). Our advice is to avoid their use unless you can be sure that the readers of your message will understand what you mean.

The next chapter shows you a simple system for organising the information you have found in your searches.

7 Information management: How to organise the information found

- *What do I do with information once I have found it?*
- *What is more important—storage or retrieval?*
- *How do I handle information that I might want to use again in the future?*

You've already spent time and effort gathering information on a topic. How you handle that information next is critical in terms of saving future time and effort. You need to organise the information as you collect it, to meet both your short-term and long-term retrieval needs. The short-term needs are those of the specific task or assignment you are currently working on—the reason for your current information quest. However, if there is a good chance you will need to find that information again, you also have a need to store and retrieve the information in the long term.

Storage and retrieval

Anyone can develop an information *storage* system. The real knack, and most important, is to develop an information *retrieval* system. Think about it in terms of your favourite

The Nerd System ™

The Much-Maligned Always-Reliable Third Information Management System

jumper. Do you put it away in a sealed box and store it under the bed and then forget about it? Or do you put it on a shelf in your wardrobe where it can be seen and easily retrieved? The whole point of storing something is so that you can retrieve it later. If you don't need to retrieve a piece of information, then you should throw it away after the first use. The information management system you choose should therefore focus on the practicality of retrieval.

What information do you store?

You have collected books and articles and scanned them for relevance—now what do you do? The essential part of any filing system for information sources is the recording of bibliographic information, such as author(s), title, year and place of publication for the books, articles or reports which you have discovered in your search. Not only are such bibliographic details important for retrieving information, but they are also necessary when you need to formally reference your information (see Chapter 9 for further detail).

There are two basic information management systems you can use:

Figure 7.1   An individual index card

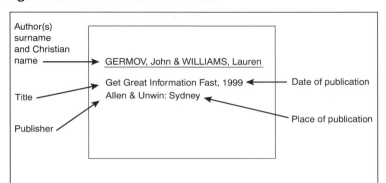

- the index card system
- the computer system.

Either system is easy to use and modify to suit both your short-term and long-term needs of organising, storing and retrieving information. The rest of the chapter takes you through each system so that you can decide the one that works best for you.

The index card system

The simplest system is the time-honoured but still effective index card system. This system is useful for people who don't have a computer or who need their system to be very portable. Packets of index cards are available fairly cheaply at newsagents in white or a variety of colours. Key bibliographic details (such as author, date, title, publisher and place) are recorded on the cards. Use one card for each piece of information you have examined, whether it be a book, book chapter, journal article, conference proceedings or video. Then retain the card in a system which makes sense to you. The card is illustrated in Figure 7.1.

The main advantage of this system is that it is cheap and easy to administer. If you record details on the cards

---

HANDY HINT 19: Identifying authors

Always err on the side of recording more information rather than less. Thus in Figure 7.1 we have recorded Christian names as well as surnames, even though in referencing you may only need the initial. Full names may help in later searches, especially in on-line catalogues.

---

in the referencing style used by your discipline (for some examples, see Chapter 9), you merely have to shuffle those cards into alphabetical or numerical order when it is time to have your bibliography or reference list typed.

The card in Figure 7.1 has all the details you need for a reference list, but you might like to store even more information, such as that included in Figure 7.2. Use one of your keywords to represent the topic and write that in the top right-hand corner—for example, 'Study Skills'. That way, you can see the topic at a glance as you flick through your cards. The extra details on the card could even be written in a different colour to clearly differentiate them from the bibliographic details—this is especially handy if you hire a typist to type up your reference list so they know which parts should be typed. When you are finished gathering information from books, you can return them to the library without having to wait to type the reference list.

Establishing your system

So far we have looked at how to record information on individual cards, and how to use those cards to type a reference list. However, for longer-term needs, if you file the cards in an organised way, you will have a quick reference database. The most beneficial use of index cards is for cataloguing journal articles (see Figure 7.3). In preparing one essay, you might collect twenty different journal

Figure 7.2 Optional extra details on your index card

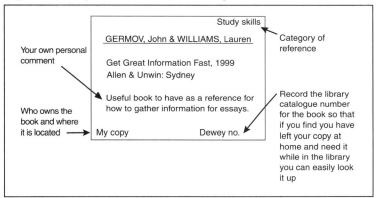

articles, using the techniques we have described in this book. If the journal article has an abstract, a quick and easy way to record the journal details is to make an extra photocopy of the abstract, cut it out and stick it on the back of the card. (You might need to reduce the photocopy to fit it on.) In this way, you'll always have a handy reminder of what the journal article was about.

Having some twenty cards handy while you are writing your essay saves you shuffling the twenty photocopied articles instead. When you come to write your essay you will have read these articles and taken notes from them. However, in writing your essay you may want to refer to studies which used a particular methodology. It is relatively quick and much less messy to check that information from the abstracts on the cards.

If you have need for any of these photocopied articles in future, these index cards can tell you where the article is stored. For example, when preparing a psychology essay on memory you photocopied an article on short-term memory degeneration. You might catalogue this as 'Memory–short-term' by writing that in the top right-hand corner of

Figure 7.3 Indexing journal articles

Study skills

GERMOV, John & WILLIAMS, Lauren

'Effective cheating skills'
The Journal of Cheating and Misbehaving,
2000, Vol. 5, No. 1, pp. 12–20.

Good, short reference to the best ways to cheat and get away with it
in a university context.

My copy   Dewey no.   See abstract overleaf

the card and filing the card in a box for psychology. That
way, if you study memory again in later years you can
quickly scan the card to see if that article will be useful to
you, rather than beginning the process of searching the
literature from scratch.

Information retrieval

As mentioned before, cataloguing needs to be done in the
most logical way for retrieval. There are several systems
you can use, the most familiar being the alphabetical
system. Using this system, you purchase alphabetical card
dividers and a card file box. Place the cards according to
the way you categorised them—for example, the card
detailing the article on memory would be filed under 'M'
for memory. A refinement of the system you might like
to consider is the use of coloured index cards. If you are
studying five different subjects in one year, you could
purchase differently-coloured cards and make each colour
represent a subject. For example, Psychology might be
yellow, Sociology pink, Philosophy blue, Economics green
and English white. You could keep the actual articles in
manila folders of the corresponding colour and file them
for future reference.

As mentioned at the outset, develop a system that

HANDY HINT 20: Avoiding a common trap: Storing your sources for future use

While you don't want to collect a continually growing mountain of material, you should throw out with caution. Courses of learning at universities and TAFEs that are longer than one year are usually designed around a body of knowledge which increases in complexity as you progress. This may not be obvious in the first year of studying for a course and, in the period of relief after exams, students may do a big clean-up and burn or 'recycle' notes and journal articles and sell textbooks, only to discover that they need to re-find the same information in later years. This means you need to develop a storage and retrieval system in the first year of your course. This doesn't mean that you need to keep every piece of paper ever collected, but it does mean you need to have a system to what you choose to keep and throw out. An each-way bet is to keep the articles you found useful for twelve months and review them to see if they are needed or have become superseded by more recent sources of information. Only if they are no longer useful and are unlikely to be useful in the future should you throw both the card and reference out (in the recycling bin).

appeals to you. You might relate better to numbers than colours and develop a numerical system.

Computer referencing systems

A more sophisticated system with almost unlimited capacity is available to those who prefer to use computers. The spreadsheet-literate can easily adapt spreadsheet programs like Microsoft© Excel and Lotus, or use database programs like Microsoft© Access5 to create records of sources

Figure 7.4   A single entry for an edited book in the Endnote program

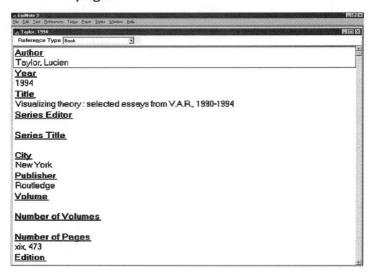

of information. However, there are also several specific software programs that enable you to catalogue books and journal articles in the way described above for index cards. Some commonly used programs are:

- **Endnote**
- **Refman**.

These programs require you to enter the key details of the article on to the computer, which creates a virtual file card, equivalent to the physical index cards described above (see Figures 7.4 and 7.5).

The biggest advantage of using these systems is that, once all the details are entered, you can generate and print your reference list or bibliography from the program—that is, there is no extra typing required. A huge benefit is that the type of referencing system you use can be changed at a keystroke. This can be very handy if you are studying subjects from

Figure 7.5   A single entry for a journal article in the Endnote program

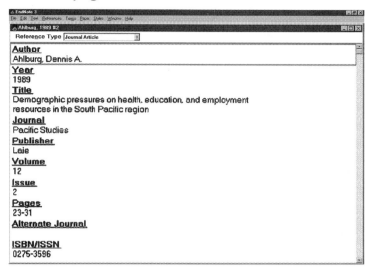

disciplines which use different systems. For example, you might have a social psychology article which you use as a reference in a psychology essay, which commonly uses the APA (American Psychological Association) system, and you then use the same article later in a social work essay which uses the Vancouver system. The other great advantage of electronic retrieval systems is that they contain powerful search tools, allowing you to retrieve lists of articles by keywords, year of publication, name of author and title.

When you are first starting out as a student it might be easiest to start with the index card system, especially until you start specialising in certain subjects. However, if you prefer to organise your work by computer and have the funds to purchase the software programs, then this method is more effective for long-term storage. Table 7.1 summarises the key features, advantages and disadvantages of the two systems.

Table 7.1 **Choosing a retrieval system**

	Card system	Computer system
Requirements	Index cards—different colours Alphabetical dividers Storage box Pen	Computer access Software access

Advantages	Inexpensive
	Simple
	Visual—can use colour coding
	Easy to delete obsolete
	  references
	Portable
	Organisation system can be
	  devised by you
		Retrieval at keystroke
		Almost unlimited capacity
		System prompts you for
		  the information to be
		  entered
		Keyword searching
		Data can be stored on
		  disk

Disadvantages	Your organisation system may
	  not lead to easy retrieval
	Lots of references can make
	  the system cumbersome
		Requires computer to
		  create and update
		Requires special software

Summary	Useful for undergraduate
	  students and short-term
	  retrieval needs
		Essential for postgraduate
		  students and long-term
		  retrieval needs

Establishing a database

So far we have talked about how to catalogue key details of references you collect for a particular purpose, such as an essay. The further you progress with your studies the more you will need an integrated information system such as a database. The term 'database' refers to an organised collection of information. It is most commonly used in referring to computers, but your database can be a paper-based system. Figure 7.6 shows an assignment for establishing a database given to final year students of Consumer Science, an Applied Science degree about food and nutrition where graduates work in a variety of settings from marketing in the food industry to health promotion.

The assignment was aimed at getting the students to establish whatever system would work for them in taking

Figure 7.6   Example of an assignment for establishing a database

---

Establishing a Nutrition Database
Collect and collate information under the following headings
- Nutrition information—scientific
- Nutrition information—industry
- Food product information
- Promotional resources—health
- Promotion resource—food
- Other (insert here however many categories are specifically relevant to you, such as health promotion, marketing, communications, etc.).

Information to be recorded
- source of data (name and address of a company, bibliographic details of a journal article, book, etc.)
- type of data available
- a critical comment about the usefulness of the data.

Process
The way in which you establish your database is up to you. Some suggestions include:

- a computerised database
- a folder with plastic sheets to store information in hard copy
- a card system kept in a file box
- whatever innovation you might come up with.

---

them from university to the employment field. Students came up with a variety of systems based on their resources and personal style. Those with home computers organised computerised databases for recording where the information was stored. Those that didn't used the card system or a loose-leaf folder system using paper and alphabetical dividers organised in a similar way to the card system. The assignment also made the students set up a corresponding system for storing the hard copies of information. Some used filing cabinets, others used cardboard file boxes (available for around $10 in larger variety stores), while others found multiple ring binders the best form of storage. They reported that finding the time to sort through all their readings and throw out those they no longer needed was the most difficult part of the task. They also felt they would have liked to have started the system in the first year of their university course. You have the opportunity to learn from their experience and start now! It is not really important what type of organisational system you choose, as long as you develop something that works for you.

Now that you have an effective management system for organising the information you have collected, the next chapter shows you how to make effective notes from that information.

8 Making effective notes and evaluating information

- *How do I find important points in sources of information?*
- *How do I write my assignment without plagiarising what others have written?*
- *How do I avoid making my summaries of information almost as long as the original source?*

In this chapter we show you how to summarise the usefulness of each piece of information you have collected in your search, how to evaluate the information you have gathered, and how to use your mind map to help clear and focus your thoughts.

In Chapter 7 you learned how to catalogue the bibliographic details of the books, reports and articles you gathered in your search. Now it's time to read more closely through these sources and to make effective notes from your reading. Before you start, you need to identify what parts of the book or journal article are relevant to your topic. If this isn't immediately obvious from the headings, you might need to skim read the book or article. Here's how to check for relevance quickly.

Skim reading

For a book, go by the headings on the contents page or index and turn to the relevant section in the text. Read the introduction and conclusion of each chapter and note the content. Also, check the preface or introduction of the book which might contain a useful summary of each chapter. When you have identified the relevant parts, read the first and last sentences of each paragraph of the section to make you aware of the scope of the section's contents. Why the first and last sentence? The first sentence of a paragraph is usually where the author outlines what they are going to discuss in the paragraph. The last sentence usually links that topic to the topic of the next paragraph. If you use this technique, be aware that what you will get is an outline of the content covered, rather than any detailed information. Let's see how well this technique works by looking at an example of the first and last sentences of a paragraph in a chapter about a health grouping known as allied health and their struggle for professional status in the health system.

> *Second, subordination affects the autonomy of the allied health professions . . . This indicates limits to professional autonomy.*

From the opening sentence we might expect that the paragraph will discuss the way in which subordination affects the autonomy of the allied health professions. From the last sentence we could expect that this discussion will link on to a further discussion of factors limiting autonomy. Now read the entire passage for yourself to check that the skimming was accurate.

> *Second, subordination affects the autonomy of the allied health professions. Autonomy is defined as control over one's own work, and has been identified by Freidson (1970) as the most important feature of professionalisation. An important question is the extent to which allied health professionals have autonomy in delivering care to patients. An Australian study looked at issues of dominance, autonomy, and author-*

ity for nursing and for four allied health professions (physiotherapy, occupational therapy, speech pathology and psychology) within the hospital setting (Kenny & Adamson 1992). They found that allied health professionals, on average, believe that they have professional autonomy, but that this was truer for practitioners with more years of experience. A staggering 20 per cent of health workers in their first year of practice did not feel able to make recommendations on patient care to referring doctors. This indicates limits to professional autonomy.

A factor limiting real autonomy is that, in the present hospital system, the ultimate responsibility for the care of the patient lies with the doctor.

(Williams, L. (1998) 'In search of profession: a sociology of allied health' in J. Germov (ed.) *Second Opinion: An Introduction to Health Sociology*, Melbourne: Oxford University Press)

You can also skim read journal articles. Most articles have abstracts, which do the work for you—you simply read the abstract which summarises the content of the article, usually in about one sentence for each section of the article. If there is no abstract, use the skimming technique and key headings to get a flavour for the content.

By the end of skimming you should be left with a pile of books and articles which contain relevant information. Those which don't look promising—either because they don't contain as much detail on the topic or because the same information is contained in other sources—you should set aside. Before you do, however, make a note on your index card or computer index system of the scope of their content if you think they might be useful for future purposes. Then return those books you aren't using currently to the library and file the articles away. Now go back to the sources that *did* look promising and read these pieces of information in more detail, starting with any secondary sources, and make notes as you go. But before you make extensive notes, it is wise to evaluate your information.

How to evaluate the information you find

How you evaluate the information you find will depend on the purpose for which it is intended, but there are a number of guidelines you should always keep in mind. As we noted in Chapter 1, it is important not to accept the information you find on face value. You can always find information about a topic, but turning that information into knowledge requires you to critically evaluate the source and content of the information. The information evaluation process comprises two stages.

In the first stage of evaluation, you determine the general relevance and credibility of the information source by checking:

* *The date and place of publication*: Determine how up to date the information is and to which country it applies.
* *The publisher*: Determine if it is a credible publishing house or has been produced by a particular corporate or political organisation which may generate bias.

**HANDY HINT 21: Unreliable sources:
Radio, television and the Internet**

There are many sources of unreliable or biased information. The way to protect yourself is always to use a number of information sources in your work, and where possible refer to the original, primary source of the information to ensure accuracy. By using a number of sources, you ensure that you encounter varied and alternative viewpoints and therefore avoid unintentional bias.

In general, unless it is specifically relevant, avoid relying solely on the media for your information, particularly radio and television programs. Tapes of radio and television programs are not easily accessible and therefore neither is any information obtained from them, which makes it difficult for people to easily verify your source. Furthermore, there are many errors of fact and opinions expressed as facts in the media (see Chapter 1).

The same caution should be applied to information obtained from the Internet. Anyone can publish information on the Internet, meaning there is plenty of misleading and inaccurate information around, along with plenty of useful information. Apply the same standards to the Internet as you would to any other source of information—judge it like you would an academic written source (see Chapters 5 and 6).

- *The perspective of the author*: Scan the contents and index pages, the references cited, and the subheadings used to determine the author's likely perspective. Always read the preface or introduction of a book, as this often summarises the author's perspective.
- *The scope of the information*: Does it address who, what, where, when and why/how?
- *The academic discipline base of the information*: This can sometimes be determined directly from the title, but also by checking the preface, introduction, concepts and

references used. This is an important criterion since a discipline-based approach may focus on particular issues and ignore those that fall outside the scope of the discipline. For example, a psychology book on management may overlook the political aspects of the topic.

The second stage of evaluating your information involves adopting an in-depth analytical approach. Depending again on the purpose for which you require the information, you should consider the following questions in determining the strengths and weaknesses of your information:

* What is the author's main argument or reason for producing the information?
* What kind of evidence is presented? Is it persuasive? Does the data support the conclusions drawn or could alternative conclusions be made?
* What key concepts, explanations and/or theories are addressed?
* Is anything left out of the author's account? Are some issues neglected? What assumptions does the author make?
* Could the author have approached the topic from another perspective? How might this have affected our understanding?
* How does the information presented relate to the issues covered in the wider literature or to the other information sources you have found?

Now that you have weeded out any sources lacking credibility, you have in front of you high-quality information from which to make notes (see HANDY HINT 21).

Making the best of your notes

Reading and note-taking are closely linked. Some people take notes as they read; others like to read first and write later. Some only highlight, rather than take notes. Our first piece

From the people that brought you
Edward Scissorhands...

Wendy Highlighterfingers

of advice is to avoid using highlighting pens in reading and note-taking. This may come as a rude shock to a lot of you—some people may need to have their highlighting pens surgically removed! Why go through such pain? Because highlighting can be one of the biggest time wasters in getting great information. Think about it. You might feel like you've done a lot of work if you highlight words or sentences as you read, but if all you end up with is a more colourful page, you haven't really achieved anything.

If you really must highlight, restrict it to direct quotes you want to use in your writing. Make a note on your index card that the article/book/chapter has a useful direct quote and note the pages. This is essential for most referencing systems which require page numbers to be cited alongside a direct quote (see Chapter 9).

HANDY HINT 22: When to take direct quotes

You should only use direct quotes when:

- the original material is expressed in a powerful, innovative, provocative or memorable way
- it is important to provide evidence supporting your interpretation of what that author said.

Keep direct quotes to a minimum. They should take up no more than 10 per cent of any written work. As a general rule, try to reword the quote in your own words first and only use it as a direct quote if it fits one of the above criteria.

If you can read without using highlighters, take notes by writing on a separate piece of paper as you read. (Some people may be able to type these notes straight on to the computer screen instead.) The risk in doing this is that you end up writing down nearly everything from the passage. This risk is intensified if you write something as you go. The quick and effective way of making notes is summarised below:

1 Skim read to determine how much of the passage is relevant to your work.
2 Take a fresh sheet of paper (or new computer screen) and write a single word or phrase which represents the topic covered in the passage. It's best if this is one of the keywords/phrases identified in the mind mapping stage of your information plan (see Chapter 2).
3 Skim through the article to get the meaning of what the author is saying.
4 Read through a small section—for example, from one sub-heading to another—or one paragraph without writing anything down. Stop reading, and consider the meaning of what the author has said.
5 In your own words, write a sentence which summarises

HANDY HINT 23: Don't forget to springboard

Note that if your essay required more than this general mention of allied health professional autonomy, you could use the chapter as a secondary source to springboard into the primary sources cited in the passage by looking up articles on the reference list of the chapter (see Chapter 2).

that section. Only look back to the passage if there are facts or technical terms you need to copy.

6   Repeat steps 4 and 5 until you are through the passage.

Let's see how this system works for the passage cited earlier. Turn back to that example on allied health practitioners. Read the paragraph. Imagine summarising it in one sentence. That sentence might look something like this:

Autonomy, or control over work, for the allied health professions is limited by subordination to medical authority in the Australian health care system (Williams 1998).

This sentence conveys the main point of the passage and is adequate as a record.

The advantage of putting each note into your own words at the time of note-taking is that you won't need to worry about plagiarising the work of another author when it comes time to reproduce the material. If you use the notes you have made, instead of the original work, the material has already been paraphrased.

As you do more reading you will build up several pages of notes. You can organise these pages in one of two ways:

1   Have a page for each keyword, and when you read something of relevance to that keyword note it down on that page no matter which piece of information it comes from, but remember to note the bibliographic details with each quote.

2 Alternatively, start a new page for each information source (that is, each article or book chapter). Write the relevant keyword at the top of each note you take. At the end, cut up each note and place it into a pile on the one topic—for example, 'Autonomy'.

Version 1 would look like this:

Autonomy:	**Subordination:**	**Gender:**	**Professionalisation strategies:**
——————— ——————— (Williams 1998) ——————— ——————— (Jerry & Adamson 1992)	——————— ——————— etc.		

Version 2 might look like this before getting cut up and placed in four separate piles:

Reading on allied health by Williams, 1998.
Autonomy:

_____
_____
✂ _____

Reading on allied health by Williams, 1998.
Subordination:

_____
_____
✂ _____

Reading on allied health by Williams, 1998.
Gender:

_____
_____
✂ _____

Reading on allied health by Williams, 1998.
Professionalisation strategies:

_____
_____

Use whichever system suits you. The aim of the exercise is for your notes to paraphrase your reading under convenient keyword headings, so that the compilation of your notes into a piece of written work is an easier and quicker process.

When you are making these notes, you might also record your own critical comments. Use a different coloured pen or font type so that you can easily recognise that they are your own comments when you come to writing up. For example:

→ *The conclusions of this author disagree with those of Smith, 1998.*

→ *This author is likely to be biased in their conclusions because of their employment.*

or

→ *This argument overlooks the fact that Australia is a multicultural society.*

→ *These conclusions are not justified given the limitations of the methodology noted by the author.*

Academic reading can be difficult and requires plenty of concentration. Some authors make it even more difficult than it needs to be by writing in a non-user-friendly style. To some extent this is because academic disciplines use jargon, and jargon can be useful as a shorthand method of communicating complicated concepts. However, many authors believe if they write too simply the work may not appear 'academic'. So don't feel disheartened if it takes you a couple of attempts to get the meaning of the passage. Mind mapping, introduced in Chapter 2 as a way to plan, can also be used to improve concentration.

Mind mapping for concentration

Mind mapping can be a useful way to clear your mind so that you can focus more clearly on your reading and note-taking. As you are no doubt aware, you can't just flip through academic sources of information like you would a magazine. You need to really concentrate on the argument and evidence presented. Mind mapping can help you to focus your thoughts—HANDY HINT 24 shows how.

HANDY HINT 24: Clearing mind clutter to focus your thoughts and concentration

Take a clean sheet of paper and draw a circle in the centre. This time, write something like:

Then quickly jot down all the individual thoughts which you will be amazed to find 'hiding' in your brain.

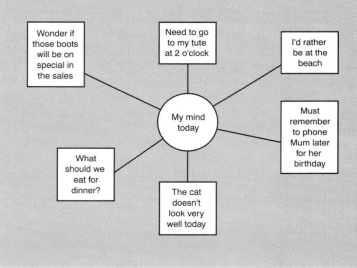

Once you get these thoughts down on paper, you can relax because you are no longer at risk of forgetting them. Your brain can trust that you will come back and deal with the issues at a later time, so they can be erased from your conscious mind—allowing you to focus on the task at hand. Keep that mind clutter map handy, though, for any other stray thoughts that pop back in.

How much is enough?

Students often ask how many pages of notes make a good assignment. The aim is for quality, but a rough guide is that you should have double the word count of the task in notes—that is, take 3000 words worth of notes for a 1500 word essay. This allows you to condense sections and get rid of repetition while cohesively linking your argument. When you find the same information coming out of several sources, you have either explored the full breadth of that key term, or you didn't collect a broad enough range of information in the early stages and you need to do some more reading.

Now that you have completed your note-taking and evaluated the information, it is time to reference your sources.

9 Referencing made easy

- *Why is referencing important? How do you reference in the Harvard/APA, footnote or Vancouver style?*
- *How do you reference the Internet?*
- *How do you reference edited books, books with no authors and newspapers?*

This chapter will take you through the basic steps of how to reference information once you have found and used it. Referencing your written work means using an accepted system to clearly identify the source of your information. Referencing consists of both making an attribution to other authors within the body of your work and then including an organised list of those references at the end. If you have followed the suggestions in Chapters 7 and 8, you should already have a basic idea of the information you need to record in order to reference properly. Now you need to conquer the different systems. Due to academic rivalry and historical legacy, there are, unfortunately, a number of different methods for referencing your work. The choice of which to use is not up to you, but is discipline-specific. For example, some disciplines use the American Psychological Association (APA) system, others use the Modern Language

HANDY HINT 25: Beware of plagiarism

Plagiarism means the theft of another author's work. It is not merely about copying an assignment from another student. It also refers to creative work, audiovisual material, software programs and written work, including the use of the same words of another author or the unacknowledged use of their concepts, theories, research findings or novel ideas. Every academic discipline will penalise you for plagiarism. Ignorance of correct referencing will not be taken as an excuse. Evidence of intention not to acknowledge or to falsely acknowledge sources is considered a serious transgression and may result in a fail or even expulsion from your study. You should also exercise the same caution for any documents or creative work that has been released in the public arena, to avoid being sued. Therefore, it is fundamentally important that you learn how to reference.

Association (MLA) method, while others prefer the footnoting technique and the sciences use the Vancouver system. This can cause confusion for students studying across disciplines—for example, a psychology student would use APA for a psychology essay, footnotes for a philosophy essay and Vancouver for a biochemistry report. Thus you need to be aware of the different systems.

This chapter will give you an overview of each of the above-mentioned referencing styles and also show you how to reference:

- books, journal articles, conference reports, CD-ROMs, films/videos and the Internet
- a number of works by the same author or authors with the same surname, published in the same year
- a number of authors on the same topic by using the 'et al.' abbreviation

- chapters written by different authors in edited books
- works with no obvious authors of the work—for example, in government reports and newspapers.

On the importance of being referenced

There are three reasons why referencing your material is important:

1 to enhance the credibility of your information (so that your assessor can check your sources)
2 to avoid plagiarism by not claiming another's work as your own (see HANDY HINT 25)
3 to allow interested readers to use your sources for further information.

What to reference

Most academic writing is about using evidence to back up your claims, whether that evidence be a theory to help explain a problem, a statistic or some detail of an event, issue or scientific research study. It might be obvious that you must reference your source when you use the direct words of another author, but it is also important to do so when you put the information into your own words. The general rule is that if the information came from an identifiable source and is not general knowledge, then you should provide a reference. This may mean that almost every paragraph in your written work may carry one or more references—this is perfectly normal and acceptable. Some sentences may even have more than one reference. You should be wary of paragraphs you write that do *not* contain a reference. It is always safer to err on the side of caution and include a reference rather than not. Referencing is your way of drawing together evidence to substantiate your argument or observations.

How to reference using the Harvard/APA citation system

The most widespread system of referencing in the humanities and social sciences is the 'author–date' system where the reference appears in brackets in the text of your written work. Simply known as the citation method, it is more commonly recognised as the Harvard or American Psychological Association (APA) reference system. It involves noting the author, date and sometimes the page number of the information source as shown in Figure 9.1.

Figure 9.1   Examples of using the citation method for in-text referencing

Germov and Williams (1996, p. 6) argue that . . .
Variations of the above could include:
Germov and Williams (1996:6)
Germov and Williams (1996, 6)

The **reference list** at the end of your assignment lists in alphabetical order (by author's surname) the full bibliographic details of the sources of information cited in your written work. For a book this includes: author's surname and initials, title (italicised or underlined), edition (where relevant), place of publication and publisher. For example:

- Germov J. and Williams L. (1999) *Get Great Information Fast*, Sydney: Allen & Unwin

For a journal article, the details included in the reference list include: author's surname and initials, article title (in single quotation marks), journal title (italicised or underlined), volume number and issue number (if relevant), and the page numbers of the article. For example, for the Germov and Williams journal article used in Figure 9.1, the reference list entry would be:

**HANDY HINT 26: Reference list or bibliography—
what's the difference?**

The list of information sources cited in the text will be called either a reference list or a bibliography depending on the academic discipline concerned. In most cases the two terms are interchangeable, but some disciplines maintain a distinction between the two terms; where a reference list is a list of the actual references cited in the text of your written work, a bibliography is a wider list of information sources related to the topic, but not specifically referenced in the text. Check the requirements in your own discipline, but unless specifically requested, it is fairly safe to assume that the only references to include in your reference list or bibliography should be the ones you actually cited in the text of your written assignment.

- Germov J. and Williams L. (1996) 'The sexual division of dieting: women's voices', *The Sociological Review*, Vol. 44, No. 4, pp. 630–47.

An alternative way to write the above reference could be:

- Germov, J. and Williams, L. 1996, The sexual division of dieting: women's voices. *The Sociological Review*, 44:4; 630–47.

Different academic disciplines and journals use variations of the citation method, in terms of whether page numbers are necessary, or how the actual reference is written in the text and in the reference list as shown above. Therefore, it is important that you learn the exact style preferred by your discipline. If no specific advice has been given, ask your lecturer which to use. You could also use the same style as common journals of your discipline.

Figure 9.2   An example of the footnote method

Allied health professions are those professions other than medicine and nursing involved in patient care.[1] While nurses make up 68% of the total health workforce and doctors make up 14%, allied health professions in total constitute 23%.[2] Germov argues that the professional claims of some allied health professions are part of a much wider challenge to medical autonomy in the health sector.[3] For Williams, the future of allied health lies in an increasing alliance between the often disparate individual health professions such as nutrition and dietetics, occupational therapy, physiotherapy and speech pathology to name a few.[4] The expertise of this group of health professions is often based on their concern for health promotion, and it is this distinctive contribution, Williams argues, that offers the greatest potential for allied health to significantly influence health policy independent of the medical profession.[5]

Note that these footnotes would literally appear at the 'foot' of the page of the text to which they correspond.

1   Williams, L. (1998) 'In search of profession: a sociology of allied health', in J. Germov (ed.), *Second Opinion: An Introduction to Health Sociology*, Melbourne: Oxford University Press, p. 293.
2   ibid., p. 294.
3   Germov, J. (1998) 'Challenges to medical dominance', in J. Germov (ed.), *Second Opinion: An Introduction to Health Sociology*, Melbourne: Oxford University Press, p. 246.
4   Williams op. cit., p. 285.
5   ibid.

Always remember to include the name of the author along with the op. cit. to avoid any confusion. When there is more than one book or article by the same author, the actual title of the publication is included along with the author's surname.

How to use the footnote method

An alternative method of referencing your material is by using footnotes. A footnote refers to the insertion of a superscript number where the reference should be; the number refers to a note printed at the foot of the page where the corresponding bibliographic details for the source of the information are listed. Footnotes are numbered consecutively. Numbers are never repeated even when starting a new page (see Figure 9.2).

> **HANDY HINT 27: Using Latin abbreviations when footnoting**
>
> The following Latin abbreviations are commonly used with the footnoting method:
>
> - ibid. (abbreviation for *ibidem*, meaning 'in the same place'): used to refer to the same reference in the previous footnote.
> - op. cit. (abbreviation for *opere citato*, meaning 'in the work cited'): used to refer to the same item already referenced earlier, but different from the one directly above it.
>
> Note that the Latin abbreviations should be in lower case roman font and that the full stops should always be included.

The first reference to a book, chapter or article in a footnote must provide full bibliographic details (as you would provide in a bibliography or reference list). After that, if the same sources are referenced again, you can use the Latin abbreviations ibid. and op. cit. (see HANDY HINT 27).

How to use the Vancouver referencing system

The Vancouver referencing system is similar to footnotes and is most commonly used in sciences, medicine, health sciences, health promotion and public health. Similar to footnoting, this system also uses numbers in the text, but the numbers are put in brackets, not superscripted. The numbers correspond to references which are placed at the end of the written work rather than at the bottom of text pages. In effect, this system combines footnotes and a reference list into one. A list of references is compiled by citing sources numbered in the order in which they appear in the text. Each source is given

Figure 9.3 An example of the Vancouver system

Allied health professions are those professions other than medicine and nursing involved in patient care(1). While nurses make up 68% of the total health workforce and doctors make up 14%, allied health professions in total constitute 23%(1). Germov claims that the professional claims of some allied health professions are part of a much wider challenge to medical autonomy in the health sector(2). For Williams, the future of allied health lies in an increasing alliance between the often disparate individual health professions such as nutrition and dietetics, occupational therapy, physiotherapy and speech pathology to name a few(1). The expertise of this group of health professions is often based in their concern for health promotion, and it is this distinctive contribution, Williams argues, that offers the greatest potential for allied health to significantly influence health policy independent of the medical profession(1).

Reference list
1   Williams L. In search of profession: a sociology of allied health. In Germov J. ed. Second Opinion: An Introduction to Health Sociology. Melbourne: Oxford University Press, 1998:281–301.
2   Germov, J. Challenges to medical dominance. In Germov J. ed. Second Opinion: An Introduction to Health Sociology. Melbourne: Oxford University Press, 1998:230–48.

only one number. This means that when a previously numbered reference is cited again, the original number is used, resulting in non-consecutive numbering of references in the text (unlike the footnote method). Each number cited in the text refers to a specific reference recorded next to that number in the reference list. Figure 9.3 provides an example of the Vancouver system.

Note from the above example that the Vancouver system does not italicise or highlight the titles of books and journals, there are no quotation marks used for article or chapter titles, and Latin abbreviations are not used. It is clear from the above example that the Vancouver system is the simplest referencing system in terms of formatting requirements; however, it can be difficult to use if you don't have an effective information management system (see Chapter 7). Things can be especially difficult if you have already numbered your references and compiled your reference list, then

> **HANDY HINT 28: Abbreviating journal titles**
>
> In the Vancouver system, journal titles are often abbreviated using a format published in the catalogue *Index Medicus* (available in your library). For example:
>
> - *The American Journal of Epidemiology* is abbreviated to *Am J Epidermoil.*
> - *The International Journal of Obesity and Related Matabolic Disorders.* becomes *Int J Obes.*
> - *American Journal of Clinical Nutrition* becomes *Am J Clin Nutr.*
>
> Note that you cannot make up your own abbreviations—if you want to use this facility, you need to look up *Index Medicus* in hard copy or on-line.

you edit out a paragraph which takes out three references, and therefore three numbers, and throws your entire system out. To avoid this, you should use the author–date citation system for in-text references as you write your drafts, and only translate the references into numbers when you are sure your piece of work is complete. Then shuffle your index cards or computerised references (as discussed in Chapter 7) according to the order in which the references occur to compile the reference list.

How to reference a number of authors on the same topic

After making notes from your information sources, you will often find there is some content overlap, where a number of different authors all basically say the same thing or agree on a particular issue. If this is the case, you can include all the different authors in the one reference in the following way:

Many studies suggest . . . (Germov and Williams 1996; Willis 1995; Sobal 1999; Ikeda 1999).

> Note that a semicolon separates the different authors

In the footnote system, the multiple references would all appear under one footnote. In the Vancouver system this would read:

Many studies suggest . . . (1–3,4)

> The first number span includes references 1 to 3; non-consecutive references are separated by a comma

How to reference direct quotes

As explained earlier, you should keep direct quotes to a minimum when writing up your notes into an assignment. However, when you do want to directly quote an author, always do the following:

- Use the exact wording of the original source.
- Place short quotes (less than 30 words) in quotation marks.
- If a quote is longer than 30 words, indent the quote from both left and right margins—when you do this there is no need to use quotation marks.
- Always include the specific page number(s) where the quote can be found.

The two examples below show how a direct quote would appear in the text of your written work using the Harvard/APA system for a short and a long quote.

Example of short, direct quote:
Williams (1998, p. 283) states that allied health professions 'can be defined as those professions (other than medicine and nursing) that are involved in patient care'.

Example of long, direct quote:
Williams (1998, p. 283) states that allied health professions

> can be defined as those professions (other than
> medicine and nursing) that are involved in patient
> care. This functionality is reflected in the organis-
> ational structures of public hospitals, where these
> professions are grouped formally or informally under
> the heading of allied health.

Note that when indenting long
quotes there is no need to use
quotation marks

How to use the et al. abbreviation

When there are more than three authors, and only then, it is
acceptable to use the Latin abbreviation et al. (short for *et allii*,
meaning 'and others') to save space. You can do this after you
have written the names out in full once. This is particularly
helpful when citing material in natural and physical science-
based disciplines where there can often be ten or more authors.

Smith et al. (1988) argue that . . .

Note the use of lower case and the full stop. The
'et al.' goes after the first author. The names of
the other authors are listed in the reference list

However, when listing Smith in the reference list, you need
to include the names of all the authors; et al. should only
be used in the text.

How to differentiate between different authors
when the surname and date are the same

You may want to use two sources written by the same author
in the same year or two sources by authors that share the

same name. If this is the case, you can distinguish your APA/Harvard in-text references by placing lower case letters next to the date of publication in the following way:

* Connell (1998a)—work written by Connell in 1998 with the letter 'a' added to distinguish the reference from another work by Connell in the same year.
* Connell (1998b)—a different work written by the same Connell in 1998 designated by the letter 'b'.

Your reference list will provide all the other bibliographic information (title, publisher and place of publication) for each Connell entry, designated by letters next to the dates. In this way, anyone can easily identify which source a reference specifically indicates. If using the footnote or Vancouver system, the references will receive different numbers in the text.

Referencing multi-authored, edited books

It is quite common to use information obtained from multi-authored, edited books, where individual chapters are written by different authors. Most people reference edited books incorrectly the first time they try, because they tend to reference the editors of the book, rather than the authors of the chapters they actually used. An example of the *wrong* way to do it is:

> Germov, J. (ed.) (1998) *Second Opinion: An Introduction to Health Sociology*, Melbourne: Oxford University Press.

An edited book

In this book there are many chapters written by different authors. Let's say you want to reference information from the following chapter within the book *Second Opinion*:

Williams, L., 'In search of profession: a sociology of allied health'.

In the text of your assignment, you would reference the actual author of the work from where you got your information—that is, you would reference Williams, not Germov. For example:

Williams (1998) maintains that . . .

> Note that the publication date is taken from the year the edited book was published

In your reference list, you would include the full details of the Williams chapter as follows:

> Note that the chapter title is placed in single quotation marks

Williams, L. (1998) 'In search of profession: a sociology of allied health', in J. Germov (ed.), *Second Opinion: An Introduction to Health Sociology*, Melbourne: Oxford University Press.

> No need to repeat the publication date here

The simple tip to remember is to always reference the author of the work you are using. Don't place the editor of a book as author, when you actually mean your material has come from a specific chapter. Always reference the author of the chapter and make sure you include the full details of the reference, including the chapter title, in your reference list. Some referencing systems also require you to list the first and last page numbers of the chapter in your reference list.

How to reference a source when there is no obvious author

Many government reports and publications produced by organisations such as the United Nations and the Organisation of Economic Cooperation and Development (OECD)

HANDY HINT 29: What is the difference between editions, impressions and reprints?

If you are using the first edition of a book, you don't need to note that it is the first edition in your reference list. However, you must always note subsequent editions of a book—for example, the second or third edition—because different editions can often mean that the content and page numbers have changed from the previous edition. If you are using a second edition, record the date that edition was printed instead of the date of the first edition.

Impressions and reprints signify the reprinting of a book because the previous print run has sold out. They should not be confused with new editions, as there is no new content and page numbers have not changed. Therefore, there is no need to note impressions or reprints in your reference list, and the date you record should be the original publication date, not the reprint date.

have no identifiable author. The rule of thumb in such cases is to reference the publisher as the de facto author (the details of which are usually found on the inside cover), which is usually the agency or department producing the document. Sometimes, government publications include a preferred way to be referenced, located on the inside cover. However, the usual case is that few reference details are given. For example, an OECD publication with no author would be referenced in the following way:

- *In your written assignment*:
  (Organisation of Economic Cooperation and Development 1998).
- *In your reference list*:
  Organisation of Economic Cooperation and Development (1998) *Economic Indicators*, Paris: Organisation of Economic Cooperation and Development.

An edition   An Impression   A Reprint

Government departments produce many publications that are often published by the one publishing agency. In this case, always reference the department as the author, unless otherwise stated. For example:

* Department of Industrial Relations (1995) *Best Practice in Action*, Canberra: Australian Government Publishing Service.
* Australian Bureau of Statistics (1997) *National Nutrition Survey: Selected Highlights*, Canberra: Australian Bureau of Statistics.

Sometimes there may be no author or publisher listed. Your only option then is to reference the title of your information source along with the year it was published. For example:

* *In your written paper:*
  (*Health Promotion Success Stories* 1998).
* *In your reference list:*
  Health Promotion Success Stories (1998) [no publication details given].

> If a reference is missing essential bibliographic material, it is acceptable to inform the reader of this. Publisher and date details are not provided in many reports

If you have a number of items with no identifiable author, group them together and list them at the start or end of your reference list for the APA/Harvard system since

HANDY HINT 30: Using suggested citations

Sometimes reports produced by organisations have a 'suggested citation' which can be found on the inside cover of these reports—use these to make life easier for you. For example, the following suggested method of referencing was included on the inside cover of the report:

Suggested citation:
Risk Factor Prevalence Study Management Committee Risk Factor Prevalence Study: Survey No. 3 1998. Canberra: National Heart Foundation of Australia and Australian Institute of Health, 1990.

they have no author to allow listing in alphabetical order. This is not an issue for the Vancouver or footnoting systems, which list in numerical order.

How to reference newspapers

Since newspapers are published regularly, you need to give the exact date of publication. Many newspaper articles do not have an author. When no author is named, reference a newspaper article in the following manner:

* *In your written paper, using the Harvard method*:
  (the *Australian* 1 April 1998, p. 10).
* *In your reference list*:
  the *Australian* 1 April 1998, p. 10.

If there is an author, then simply follow the normal procedure—that is:

* *In your written paper, using the Harvard method*:
  (Smith 1998, p. 10).
* *In your reference list*:
  Smith, Z. (1998) 'Back pain: a personal journey', the *Australian* 1 April, p. 10.

How to reference unusual sources: conference papers, CD-ROMs and films/videos

You may come across volumes of conference papers, which are publications of the papers presented at particular academic conferences. These should be treated in a similar way to edited books (described above) except that you need to note the exact date and place of the conference. For example:

- Coveney, J. (1998) 'Moral positions in public health nutrition: the relevance of Michel Foucault', in *Nutrition Unplugged: Back to Basics. Proceedings of the 16th Dietitians Association of Australia National Conference*, Hobart, 14–17 May.

> *Note:* Conference volumes often have no explicit editor

The general rule of thumb for referencing material published on CD-ROMs is to treat them like books, ensuring to include the publisher/production company and to note that the source is a CD-ROM in your actual reference. For example:

- Australian Family Resources [CD-ROM] (1994), Melbourne: Australian Institute of Family Studies in association with the Royal Melbourne Institute of Technology.

If you need to reference a video or film, state the title, followed by the date, the production company, the place of production and the running time. If there is more than one video in the series, state which volume you used. For example:

- *The Politics of Food* (1987), Yorkshire Television, Leeds, Vol. 4, 52 minutes.

Internet referencing

This section will explain the correct technique of referencing information found on the Internet. The general principle to

HANDY HINT 31: Internet copyright and plagiarism

It is easy to copy images off the Internet on to your computer. Similarly, you can copy and paste slabs of written material with a few manoeuvres of the mouse. However, such convenience can lead to bad habits, such as plagiarism and copyright infringement. Direct usage of written material, whether from an electronic academic journal, a downloaded document or simply a person's web site, requires clear acknowledgment of the source—otherwise you are guilty of plagiarism (that is, stealing another person's work and claiming it as your own). Furthermore, if you wish to use artwork, graphics or other images you find on the Internet, seek permission. Always assume that copyright applies even if the web site is in another country.

keep in mind is to follow the conventional standard of referencing material in your academic discipline. A number of examples are provided below for different types of Internet information sources.

Referencing web pages

The idea of any referencing system is to provide enough detail so that other people can find the source of information cited. For web pages, you should aim to include (where available) the author of the information (a person, group or organisation), the date (most web pages have a date at the bottom of the page), title followed by the description 'web page' to indicate the type of Internet source, URL and the date you accessed the web page. It is important to include the access date, as web information is prone to constant change and sometimes to disappear altogether. For example, the reference for a web page would appear in your reference list as follows:

- Germov, J. and Williams, L. (1998) *Social Appetite Web* [web page], http://www.newcastle.edu.au/department/so/ socialappetite.htm, date accessed: 1 January 2000.

Some web pages include two dates, one for when the web page was established and another for when it was 'last modified'—always use the most recent date for your reference. If no author information is listed on the web page, you would simply write the reference as follows:

- *Get Great Information Fast* (1999) [web page], http://www.allen-unwin.com.au/study/infofast.htm, date accessed: 1 January 2000.

Referencing articles in electronic journals

As discussed in Chapter 4, electronic journals, or e-journals, are increasing in popularity. Some journals are solely available via the web, while most are web versions of existing hard-copy journals. When referencing an article from an e-journal, you should aim to use the following format:

- Germov, J. (1996) 'All manners of food: eating and taste in England and France from the Middle Ages to the present by Stephen Mennell' (book review), *Sociological Research Online* [e-journal], http://www.socresonline.org.uk/socresonline/1/2/germov.html, date accessed: 9 August 1998.

In the case of the above e-journal, full-length articles are segmented into numbered paragraphs, which makes it easy to specifically reference direct quotes. In most cases, however, you will not be able to provide page numbers for e-journal articles and other Internet documents. The actual URL and the date you accessed the web site are the most important pieces of information to include in web referencing.

Referencing downloaded documents

Many organisations provide you with access to download key documents such as reports and policies. In most cases, these documents will come with information on author, date, title, publisher and often include page numbers, and should therefore be referenced as a normal hard-copy document, along with the URL and the date accessed.

Referencing e-mail

In general, e-mail is a personal communication and should rarely be used as a source. However, if you need to reference information contained in an e-mail, always seek permission from the person who sent the e-mail and never record the actual e-mail address in the reference, for privacy reasons. Always print and keep a copy of the e-mail you are referencing as evidence of the source of the information just in case evidence is requested. To reference an e-mail that is a personal communication (pers. comm.) between yourself and another person, you can use the following format which clearly identifies the specific date and that the source is from an e-mail:

- Germov, J. (1998) pers. comm. [e-mail], 12 December.

Referencing mailing lists and Usenet newsgroups

While some lists and all newsgroups do archive their messages by topic or theme, the transitory nature of such information means it is unlikely that other people will be able to access it. Generally, you should avoid referencing information from such sources due to their lack of credibility. However, if you need to do so, use the following format:

- Williams, L. (1997) 'How to reference newsgroups', comp.getinfo.www.users [Usenet newsgroup], date accessed: 20 December 1998.

HANDY HINT 32: Automatically switching between referencing systems

Chapter 7 provides examples of computer programs that allow you to store your references and automatically generate a reference list or instantly convert your reference style from one format to another—for example, from footnotes to the APA system. These programs are worth the investment if your work entails using a number of different referencing systems.

Note that in the above example, the actual message was archived in the particular list in 1997, but accessed at a different date.

Choose your referencing system

This chapter has provided you with the basics of how to reference within the text and produce a reference list. It is now up to you to check the specific requirements of your particular academic discipline. There are many referencing guides available that provide further help with referencing (see Chapter 2 for a list of some).

Now that you have completed your reference list, you are ready to move on to writing your essay, report or assignment. Good luck! The final chapter provides some examples of how to apply your information to various types of assignments.

10 The information quest: Where to from here?

I like to do my principal research in bars, where people are more likely to tell the truth or, at least, lie less convincingly than they do in briefings and books.

P.J. O'Rourke (1988) *Holidays in Hell,* New York: Vintage Books, p. 227.

An overview of your information quest

If you have followed the steps in this book, by now you will have great information that is organised and appropriate for the task at hand. Figure 10.1 outlines the key features of the steps that we have covered in various chapters. We have called this step-by-step approach the Information Search Plan (ISP). The stages involved in the ISP show the importance of a systematic approach to searching for information. By following the various stages, you will be able to save time and improve the quality of the information you find.

Applying the information you have found

How you handle that information now depends on the reason for your search in the first place.

Figure 10.1 The eight stages of the Information Search Plan

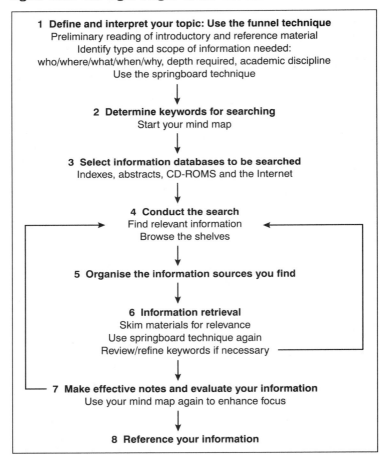

1 **Define and interpret your topic: Use the funnel technique**
Preliminary reading of introductory and reference material
Identify type and scope of information needed:
who/where/what/when/why, depth required, academic discipline
Use the springboard technique

2 **Determine keywords for searching**
Start your mind map

3 **Select information databases to be searched**
Indexes, abstracts, CD-ROMS and the Internet

4 **Conduct the search**
Find relevant information
Browse the shelves

5 **Organise the information sources you find**

6 **Information retrieval**
Skim materials for relevance
Use springboard technique again
Review/refine keywords if necessary

7 **Make effective notes and evaluate your information**
Use your mind map again to enhance focus

8 **Reference your information**

• *Writing an essay*
The steps you have followed have put you well on the
way to completing your essay—by finding great information. Your note-taking and evaluation will form the
first draft of your essay, and your reference list should
already be in order. You may require more specific

information on essay writing if you find it difficult or you are in a degree program for which the main type of assessment task is an essay. The companion to this book, *Get Great Marks for Your Essays* by John Germov (published by Allen & Unwin), is a user-friendly guide to essay writing. Your academic discipline or university may also provide essay writing guides.

*   *Writing a project report or laboratory report*
    These pieces of work are usually specific tasks that follow a particular style for each discipline. The scientific report, on which a laboratory report is based, will follow the general outline:
    Introduction: The background science which introduces the experiment to be conducted.
    Methods: A detailed description of exactly how you conducted the experiment (written in the past tense).
    Results: A detailed description of your findings (also written in the past tense) which you may describe in written, tabular and graphical forms.
    Discussion: Analysis of what your findings mean in the light of what we already know.
    Conclusion: A final statement summarising the main finding from the experiment and suggesting a direction for further research.
    Read your subject or laboratory handout carefully for instructions on how to complete laboratory reports in your discipline. If there are no such instructions, ask your lecturer or laboratory demonstrator for details.

*   *Writing a thesis or dissertation*
    Research projects and higher degrees require more substantial publications that vary from discipline to discipline. A description of how to undertake these tasks is outside the scope of this book, but there are several good books on the market. Another useful practice is to borrow a thesis already completed within your discipline and read it for scope and layout more so than for the

content. Your supervisor will have copies of previous theses, but copies are also usually available from the library.

- *Literature review*
  A literature review is similar to an essay, but it focuses on one particular topic. The aim is to review all that has been written on a topic—for example, public sector reform—in order to come to a conclusion about what we already know, and to indicate where further research is needed.

- *Debate or oral presentation*
  These types of presentations usually rely on you to mount an argument supported by facts. Part of your assessment will be based on the accuracy of your content and the persuasiveness of your argument. You can enhance your marks in this area by using the techniques for getting great information in this book. However, the rest of your mark will be based on your presentation or debating skills. These are important to develop but are outside the scope of this book. If you lack confidence about standing up and presenting in front of others, you may need to do extra courses to improve your skills. Such courses are often available through your university learning skills unit, through community adult education courses and through organisations such as Toastmasters.

All of the above tasks rely on your writing skills. This book has focused on how to gather information; now you need to present that information in writing. If you have writer's block, you can use the mind mapping technique to clear your mind of clutter, as described in Chapter 8. But if it is written expression itself that you have a problem with, you will need to do some extra work to master this important skill. Most universities run free workshops on writing skills, which you should take advantage of. Some learning skills units may also offer one-on-one tutoring where

HANDY HINT 33: By the end of this book you should be . . .

- able to determine the nature and scope of the information you require (Chapter 1)
- aware of key sources of information to interpret your topic (Chapter 2)
- familiar with the physical layout of your library (Chapter 3)
- able to use the on-line catalogue both in the library and remotely (Chapter 3)
- in possession of printed discipline-specific search help guides (Chapter 3)
- competent at on-line database searching for journals (Chapter 4)
- capable of using Boolean operators to expand or narrow your keyword searches (Chapter 4)
- able to search the web effectively, reference the web and use some time-saving short cuts to find high-quality information (Chapter 5)
- able to subscribe to 'push' information services in your key research areas (Chapter 5)
- able to find relevant mailing lists and Usenet news-groups (Chapter 6)
- competent at organising your information by using an index system suitable to your needs (Chapter 7)
- aware of the skim-reading technique, how to make effective notes and how to evaluate the information you have found (Chapter 8)
- able to reference different sources of information (Chapter 9).

you take a piece of work you have written for comments on your grammar, expression and so on. Most lecturers will not correct grammar in drafts, since they operate on the general expectation that you learned correct English expression at school. This can make things especially difficult if

English is your second language; again, you need to take advantage of any support services offered.

The quest for information is a never-ending process of search and discovery. However, we are confident that you now have the skills and knowledge to get great information fast. HANDY HINT 33 serves as a final reminder of what any information quest involves. If there are any areas you need to brush up on, go back to the relevant chapters before undertaking your next task.

The appendix provides a list of relevant web sites as a convenient starting-point for conducting web research.

Appendix Key sites for getting started on the web

All the web addresses listed throughout this book are listed here for your convenience. We have also listed other sites that are good launching points for conducting web research. Since web addresses change often, the easiest place to start is with the *Get Great Information Fast* web page, where we provide an up-to-date list of links to all of the sites listed below.

Get Great Information Fast web page

http://www.allen-unwin.com.au/study/infofast.htm

Directories and search engines

All-in-one search sites

All-in-One: http://www.albany.net.allinone
CNet Search.com: http://search.cnet.com
Internet Sleuth: http://www.isleuth.com
Webtaxi: http://www.webtaxi.com

E-mail directories

Bigfoot: http://www.bigfoot.com
Four 11: http://www.four11.com

Internet Address Finder: http://www.iaf.net
WhoWhere?: http://www.whowhere.com

Mailing list and Usenet newsgroup directories

DejaNews: http://www.dejanews.com
Liszt: http://www.liszt.com
Mailbase: http://www.blpes.lse.ac.uk/internet/beginners
Publicly Accessible Mailing Lists:
http://www.neosoft.com/internet/paml
Reference.Com: http://www.reference.com
Search the Net: http://www.statsvet.uu.se/maillist.html
Talkway: http://www.talkway.com/usenet

Meta-index search engines

Dogpile: http://www.dogpile.com
Inference Find: http://www.inference.com/ifind
Internet Sleuth: http://www.isleuth.com
MetaCrawler: http://www.go2net.com/search.html
Metafind: http://www.metafind.com
SavvySearch: http://www.savvysearch.com
W3 Search Engines:
http://osiris.sunderland.ac.uk/rif/W3searches.html

Phone and address directories

PhoneNumbers.Net: http://www.phonenumbers.net
Switchboard (US): http://www.switchboard.com
Telstra Springboard:
http://www.springboard.telstra.com.au/directories/global.htm

Search engines

Altavista: http://www.altavista.digital.com
Excite: http://www.excite.com
Hotbot: http://www.hotbot.com
InfoSeek: http://www.infoseek.com
Search Engine Watch: http://www.searchenginewatch.com

Subject directories

Anzwers Search Centre: http://www.anzwers.com.au
Ask Jeeves: http://www.askjeeves.com
The Argus Clearinghouse: http://www.clearinghouse.net
Encyclopaedia Britannica Internet Guide: http://www.eblast.com
InfoPlease: http://www.Infoplease.com
InfoSeek Guide: http://www.infoseek.com
The Internet Public Library: http://www.ipl.org
LookSmart: http://www.looksmart.com.au
Lycos: http://www.lycos.com
Magellan: http://www.mckinley.com
Netscape Australian Guide:
http://home.netscape.com/au/escapes/search/netsearch_O.html
Suite101: http://www.suite101.com
WWW Virtual Library: http://www.w3.org/vl
Yahoo: http://www.yahoo.com.au

Alphabetical listing

Art galleries and museums

The Electronic Library: http://www.books.com/scripts/lib.exe
The Louvre: http://mistral.culture.fr/louvre
Metropolitan Museum of Art, New York City:
http://www.metmuseum.org
Museums Around the World: http://www.icom.org/vimp/world.html
Smithsonian Institution: http://www.si.edu
WebMuseum: http://netcity.netspot.com.au/wm/index.html
Worldwide Arts Resources: http://www.wwar.com/museums.html

Bookstores

Amazon.com: http://www.amazon.com
Barnes and Noble: http://www.barnesandnoble.com
Bookwire: http://www.bookwire.com
The Coop Bookshop: http://www.coop-bookshop.com.au
Internet Public Library: http://www.ipl.org

Rare, used and out-of-print books

Bibliofind: http://www.bibliofind.com
BookSearch: http://www.booksearch.com

Business and finance

Austrade (Australian Trade Commission):
http://www.austrade.gov.au
Australian Competition and Consumer Commission:
http://www.accc.gov.au/index.htm
Australian Consumers Association: http://www.choice.com.au
Australian Securities and Investments Commission:
http://www.asic.gov.au
Australian Stock Exchange: http://www.asx.com.au
Business Index: http://www.dis.strath.ac.uk/business
Industry Commission: http://www.indcom.gov.au

Computing

HotWired: http://www.hotwired.com
NetGuide: http://www.netguide.com/home
Yahoo Computing: http://www.yahoo.com/computers

Cultural links, film and television

All Movie Guide: http://www.allmovie.com
Australia's Cultural Network: http://www.acn.net.au
Internet Movie Database: http://www.imdb.com

Education on-line

AskERIC: http://ericir.sys.edu
Open Learning Australia: http://www.ola.edu.au
Studylink (on-line tertiary education links):
http://www.studylink.com.au
UltiBASE: http://ultibase.rmit.edu.au
World Lecture Hall: http://www.utexas.edu/world/lecture/index.html

E-journals and e-zines

E-journal directories:
http://www.aph.gov.au/library/intguide/gen/genejrnl.htm
E-zine List: http://www.meer.net/~johnl/e-zine-list
The Internet Public Library on-line serials page:
http://www.ipl.org/reading/serials
NewJour: http://gort.ucsd.edu/newjour
Salon: http://www.salonmag.com
UnCover: http://uncweb.carl.org

Gender and feminism

Femina: http://www.femina.cybergrrl.com
The Feminist Majority Foundation: http://www.feminist.org
National Women's Justice Coalition:
http://www.ozemail.com.au/~nwjc
WEL: Women's Electoral Lobby: http://www.pcug.org.au/other/wel
Women's Guide to the Internet:
http://www.fastlink.com.au/clients/ccafe/women.html

Government

Embassies and consulates:
http://www.escapeartist.com/embassy1/embassy1.htm
Governments of the world: http://www.hg.org/govt.html
Governments on the WWW: http://www.gksoft.com/govt/en
Governments on the web: http://www.aph.gov.au/library/intguide/geog
Australian government: http://www.fed.gov.au
Australian federal and state government links:
http://www.aph.gov.au/library/intguide/gen/genausg.htm
New Zealand: http://www.govt.nz
Canada: http://canada.gc.ca/main_e.html
UK: http://www.open.gov.uk
US: FedWorld: http://www.fedworld.gov

Health and medicine

Achoo: http://www.achoo.com
AEGIS (HIV/AIDS information): http://www.aegis.com

Australia & New Zealand Food Authority: http://www.anzfa.gov.au

Australian Institute of Health and Welfare: http://www.aihw.gov.au

EurekAlert: http://www.eurekalert.org

Food and Drug Administration: http://www.fda.gov

Health on the Net: http://www.hon.ch/home.html

MedWeb: http://www.medwebplus.com

National Centre for Epidemiology and Population Health: http://www-nceph.anu.edu.au

National Health and Medical Research Council: http://www.health.gov.au/nhmrc

National Institutes of Health: http://www.nih.gov

National Library of Medicine (USA, includes free access to Medline): http://www.nlm.nih.gov

New York Academy of Medicine: http://www.nyam.org

NursingNet: http://www.nursingnet.com

Public Health Association: http://www.pha.org.au

Reuters Health: http://www.reutershealth.com

Uniserve Health: http://health.uniserve.edu.au

Women's Health Australia: http://u2.newcastle.edu.au/wha

World Health Organization: http://www.who.org

Humanities and social sciences

American Psychological Association Psychnet: http://www.apa.org

Asia-Pacific Centre for Human Resource and Development Studies: http://www.fec.newcastle.edu.au/~apc/index.html

Australian Institute of Family Studies: http://www.aifs.org.au

The Australian Sociological Association: http://www.newcastle.edu.au/department/so/tasa

The English Pages: http://longman.awl.com/englishpages

Envirolink: http://www.envirolink.org

ESRC Economic and Social Research Council (UK): http://www.esrc.ac.uk

HNET (Humanities and Social Science Online): http://h-net2.msu.edu

HyperHistory (world history):
http://www.hyperhistory.com/online_n2/History_n2/a.html
The Scout Report: http://scout.cs.wisc.edu/scout/report/index.html
Social Policy Research Centre: http://www.sprc.unsw.edu.au
Sociological Research Online: http://www.socresonline.org.uk
SOSIG: Social Science Information Gateway:
http://sosig.ac.uk
Useful Web Resources for Social Scientists:
http://www.socresonline.org.uk/socresonline/3/2/holbrook.html

Industrial relations

ACIRRT: Australian Centre for Industrial Relations,
Research & Training: http://www.econ.usyd.edu.au/acirrt
Australian Industrial Relations Commission:
http://www.airc.gov.au
ESC: Employment Studies Centre: http://u2.newcastle.edu.au/esc
Evatt Foundation: http://www.peg.apc.org/~evatt
National Key Centre for Industrial Relations:
http://www.buseco.monash.edu.au/Centres/NKCIR

International organisations

Amnesty International: http://www.amnesty.org
APEC (Asia-Pacific Economic Cooperation):
http://www.apecsec.org.sg
EU (European Union): http://www.europa.eu.int
G7 Implementation Group: http://www.g7sig.org
Greenpeace International: http://www.greenpeace.org
IMF (International Monetary Fund): http://www.imf.org
NATO (North Atlantic Treaty Organisation): http://www.nato.int
OECD (Organisation for Economic Co-operation and Development): http://www.oecd.org
United Nations list of international organisations:
http://www.unsystem.org/index5.html
World Bank: http://www.worldbank.org
WTO: World Trade Organisation: http://www.wto.org

Law

Attorney-General's Department web site: http://www.law.gov.au
Australasian Legal Information Institute:
http://www.austlii.edu.au
Australian Law Reform Commission: http://www.alrc.gov.au
International law links: http://www.aph.gov.au/library/intguide/law
National Women's Justice Coalition: http://www.nwjc.org.au

Libraries

Australian university libraries:
http://www.anu.edu.au/caul/uni-libs.htm
The Internet Public Library: http://www.ipl.org
Librarians' Index to the Internet:
http://sunsite.berkeley.edu/internetindex
Libweb (libraries of the world): http://sunsite.berkeley.edu/Libweb
National Library of Australia: http://www.nla.gov.au
National Library of Canada: http://nlc-bnc.ca
National Library of New Zealand: http://www.natlib.govt.nz
Portico—British Library's Online Service: http://portico.bl.uk
USA Library of Congress: http://lcweb.loc.gov
USA National Library of Medicine: http://www.nlm.nih.gov

News media

Yahoo provides a handy international news headlines service.
On a daily basis, major news items from around the world
are indexed. By clicking on a specific story or topic, you
are taken to a list of story headlines, including the source
and the date of the material. The full text of each news
story can then be accessed.
Yahoo! News Headlines: http://dailynews.yahoo.com/headlines
The State Library of New South Wales also offers users
a service called Infoquick, which is an indexed database of
articles appearing in the *Sydney Morning Herald* from 1988
onwards. The library also provides Infokoori, an indexed

database of articles appearing in the *Koori Mail*. These services can be accessed on the web at:

Infokoori: http://www.slnsw.gov.au/koori
Infoquick: http://awairs.slnsw.gov.au/infoquick
Koori Mail: http://www.nor.com.au/media/kmail

General media links

Media Internet Resources:
http://www.aph.gov.au/library/intguide/media
Newspaper web sites: http://www.ipl.org/reading/news
Australian newspapers on the Internet:
http://www.nla.gov.au/oz/npapers.html
ABC News: http://www.abc.net.au
The Age: http://www.theage.com.au
The Australian: http://www.theaustralian.com.au
Australian Financial Review: http://www.afr.com.au
CNN: http://www.cnn.com
Electronic Newsstand: http://www.enews.com
The Guardian Online: http://www.guardian.co.uk
Multimedia Newsstand: http://www.mmnewsstand.com
New York Times: http://www.nytimes.com
Pathfinder: http://www.pathfinder.com
PointCast: http://www.pointcast.com
Reuters: http://www.reuters.com
The Sydney Morning Herald: http://www.smh.com.au
Wall Street Journal: http://www.wsj.com
The Wire (The Associated Press):
http://www.sj-r.com/news/wire/apwire.htm
Worldwide news: http://www.worldwidenews.com/worldnew.htm

Politics

Australian Electoral Commission:
http://www.aec.gov.au/next_elec/main.htm
Politics Internet Resources (Parliamentary Library of Australia):
http://www.aph.gov.au/library/intguide/pol

Major political parties
Australia:
Australian Democrats: http://www.democrats.org.au
Australian Labor Party: http://www.alp.org.au
Liberal Party: http://www.liberal.org.au
National Party: http://www.npa.org.au
New Zealand:
Political parties: http://www.parliament.govt.nz/politics-news.html
United Kingdom:
Conservative Party: http://www.conservative-party.org.uk
Labour Party: http://www.labour.org.uk
Liberal Democrats: http://www.libdem.org.uk
United States:
Democrats: http://www.democratic-party.org
Republicans: http://www.townhall.org

Reference information sites

The best one-stop web site for all your reference information
needs is My Virtual Reference Desk. It is impossible to
describe the range of information available, but it is hard to
think of something that is missing from this site. This is a
free service, well organised, easy to navigate and highly
recommended:
My Virtual Reference Desk: http://www.refdesk.com

General reference links
Bartlett's Quotations:
http://www.cc.columbia.edu/acis/bartleby/bartlett
CIA World Fact Book: http://www.odci.gov/cia/publications/pubs
Librarians' Index to the Internet:
http://sunsite.berkeley.edu/internetindex
Megaconverter (calculators for weights, measures and all
other units of measurement):
http://www.megaconverter.com/Cv_start.htm
Research-It: http://www.itools.com/research-it/research-it.html
Roget's Thesaurus: http://www.thesaurus.com

Strunk's Elements of Style:
http://www.columbia.edu/acis/bartleby/strunk
Thesaurus and Quotations: http://www.refdesk.com/factquot.html
Webpedia: http://www.webpedia.com
Yahoo Reference listings: http://www.yahoo.com/reference
Yahoo Encyclopaedia listings:
http://www.yahoo.com/reference/encyclopedia

Science

Discover magazine: http://www.discover.com
EurekAlert: http://www.eurekalert.org
MapQuest (worldwide atlas that provides street-level detail):
http://www.mapquest.com
NASA: http://www.nasa.gov
New Scientist: http://www.newscientist.com
Northern Lights (Aurora Borealis):
http://www.uit.no/npt/homepage-npt.en.html
Popular Science—PopSci: http://www.popsci.com
Skeptics: http://www.skeptics.com.au
Uniserve Engineering: http://engineering.uow.edu.au
Uniserve Science: http://www.usyd.edu.au/su/SCH
Web-Elements (elementary table): http://www.webelements.com

Software sites

Browser Watch: http://www.browserwatch.com
Cool Tools: http://www.cooltool.com
Download.com: http://www.download.com
Shareware Top 20: http://www.clicked.com.shareware
TUCOWs: http://www.tucows.com

Statistics

Many countries have a national organisation dedicated to collecting and publishing statistics. For example, the Australian Bureau of Statistics (ABS) collects and publishes volumes of statistical material on almost every topic, from census information to social indicators and commercial trade information. Statistical information is increasingly being made available via the web:

For Australian statistics, try:

ABS: http://www.statistics.gov.au

AusInfo: http://www.agps.gov.au

Australian Institute of Family Studies (AIFS):
http://www.aifs.org.au

Australian Institute of Health and Welfare (AIHW):
http://www.aihw.gov.au/contents.html

Reserve Bank of Australia Bulletin:
http://www.rba.gov.au/rbahome.html

For international statistics, try:

FastFacts: http://www.refdesk.com/fastfact.html

International statistics links:
http://www.cbs.nl/en/services/nsi-links.htm

OECD: http://www.oecd.org

United Nations: http://www.unsystem.org

US Census Bureau: http://www.census.gov

World Health Organization: http://www.who.org

Unions

ACTU (Australian Council of Trade Unions):
http://www.actu.asn.au

American Federation of Labor–Congress of Industrial
Organizations (AFL–CIO) http://www.aflcio.org/home.htm

Global Labournet: http://www.labourstart.org

ILO (International Labour Organisation):
http://www.ilo.org/public/english/index.htm

Union Web Ring:
http://www.webring.org/cgi-bin/webring?ring=unionring;list

Labornet: http://www.igc.org/igc/labornet

Universities

Australian Universities: http://www.avcc.edu.au/avcc/uniwebs.htm

Australian university library web sites:
http://www.anu.edu.au/caul/uni-libs.htm

Universities on the web:
http://www.mit.edu:8001/people/cdemello/univ.html

Web rings

Web ring home page: http://www.webring.org

Glossary

bibliographic information The information used to catalogue material, which usually includes: author, title, date of publication, place of publication, publisher, format (hard or electronic copy).

bibliography *see* Reference list

bookmark A feature all browsers provide that allows you to record and retrieve web addresses.

Boolean operators When you have more than one keyword, you can use the computer terms to limit or broaden a search request when using web search engines and electronic library catalogues:

- AND: narrows the scope of a search to a combination of specific items by retrieving only items with both terms.
- OR: broadens a search by commanding the retrieval of items with both or either term.
- NOT: limits a search by excluding terms.

See Chapter 4 for examples of using Boolean operators. *See also* Proximity operators.

browser A software program, such as Netscape and Internet Explorer, used to access the web.

CD-ROM An abbreviation for Compact Disk Read Only Memory, meaning information stored on the disk can only be read and not added to or changed in any way.

e-journals An abbreviation for electronic journals that are accessible via the web.

e-mail An abbreviation for electronic mail.

Endnote A computer software program that enables you to catalogue bibliographic information.

File Transfer Protocol (FTP) A software program that allows you to transfer files from one computer to another.

Frequently Asked Questions (FAQ) An abbreviation commonly used in e-mail discussion lists such as Usenet newsgroups. It generally refers to a file that contains answers to common questions that have been submitted to the discussion list, to avoid their repetition.

gopher A means of accessing information via the Internet, based on a hierarchical organisation of information into parent directories and sub-directories which is gradually being replaced by the more user-friendly web.

'hits' Internet slang that refers to the number of matches when doing a web search.

home page The first screen you see displayed when your browser retrieves information from a web address.

http An abbreviation for hyper-text transfer protocol, the computer language used to access the web.

hyper-text Pre-programmed web addresses that allow you to roam around the web in an easy, non-linear way by clicking on highlighted text or graphics with your computer mouse.

index and abstract databases Index and abstract databases are information directories that provide full bibliographic details such as author, date, title, volume, issue and page numbers of published material in a particular field. Abstract directories include an abstract or paragraph summary of individual articles of information.

information technology (IT) A general term used to describe electronic forms of storing, searching and retrieving information, such as on-line library catalogues, CD-ROMs and the World Wide Web.

Internet An abbreviation for international network, it describes the ability of computers to exchange information through the global telecommunications system. The Internet consists of the web, e-mail, mailing lists, Usenet newsgroups, Gopher, ftp and Telnet.

keywords Words which relate to concepts, authors and theories relevant to the topic on which you wish to gather information. See Chapter 2 for examples.

mailing lists A form of group e-mail that allows you to send an e-mail message to one address that is then re-sent to all the people who have subscribed to the mailing list.

mind map A mind map is a technique for brainstorming a topic by writing any ideas you can think of on a sheet of paper, starting with the main topic circled in the middle of the page. See Chapter 2 for examples.

netiquette Internet etiquette—the dos and don'ts of electronic communication.

plagiarism The use of another author's work without proper acknowledgment.

primary sources The original source of information, such as creative work, research data, laboratory experiments, annual reports, minutes of meetings, new concepts and theories.

proximity operators When you have more than one keyword, you can use the computer terms NEAR and NEXT to refine your search by asking an electronic search engine or library catalogue to search for keywords next to each other or near each other in a document. *See also* Boolean operators.

reference list A list of the bibliographic details of the information sources used in written work.

Refman A computer software program that enables you to catalogue bibliographic information.

review articles Articles or book chapters that provide systematic overviews of specific topics.

secondary sources Information sources that summarise, review, discuss and analyse primary source material, such as textbooks, review articles and encyclopaedias.

Telnet An abbreviation for telecommunications network, it is a software program that enables a computer to connect to another to access databases at a remote location.

URL An abbreviation for Uniform Resource Locator, which is an address of a web site that tells your browser where to search the Internet to locate a particular web site.

Usenet newsgroups Usenet is an abbreviation for User's Network. Newsgroups are like bulletin boards, organised around specific subjects, where anyone can post a message to the group and anyone can read it if they choose. When a number of people post messages responding to one another on a certain issue, this line of e-mail discussion is called a 'thread'.

virtual library Using a virtual library means using the facilities of a library without being in the actual building, through the use of information technology.

WWW An abbreviation for World Wide Web, or simply the web, it is a means for transmitting information in a variety of formats—text, graphics, animation, audio and video.

Index